The
Performing
Artist's
HANDBOOK

The Performing Artist's HANDBOOK

Janice Papolos

Writer's Digest Books

Cincinnati, Ohio

Chapter 8 and part of Chapter 1 of this book were previously published, in slightly different form, in *American Ensemble* (now *Chamber Music Magazine*). Copyright 1982 by Chamber Music America. Reprinted with permission.

Library of Congress Cataloging in Publication Data

Papolos, Janice.
The performing artist's handbook.

Bibliography: p.
Includes index.
1. Music—Vocational guidance—Handbooks, manuals, etc.
I. Title.
ML3795.P16   1984   780'.23   84-3671
ISBN 0-89879-143-X

Design by Christine Aulicino.

For my parents and Demitri;
and for Rosalie and Rosa

Behind the storm of daily conflict and crisis, the dramatic confrontations, the tumult of political struggle, the poet, the artist, the musician, continues the quiet work of the centuries, building bridges of experiences between peoples, reminding man of the universality of his feelings and desires and despairs, and reminding him that the forces that unite are deeper than those that divide.

—*John F. Kennedy*

CONTENTS

SECTION I: GETTING STARTED

SECTION II: ON YOUR WAY

ACKNOWLEDGMENTS

I am deeply indebted to the following professionals who generously gave of their time and expertise: Kristine Ciesinski, Aaron Frankel, Scott Franz, Phyllis and Robert Franz, Nick Granito, Timothy S. Jensen, Esq., Sylvia Kahan, Lydia Kontos, Michael Lobel, Gary Posner, Doug Siegel, Nancy Shear, Barbara Solomon, Kevin Walz, Barbara Walz, and Van Williams.

I would also like to thank Oscar Collier and Lisa Collier Cool for recognizing an idea, and Carol Cartaino and Howard I. Wells III for gently pulling it into reality. A very special thank you to my fine and perceptive editor, Barbara O'Brien.

And finally, I wish to acknowledge the people who stood by me and offered their considerable wisdom and good counsel: Mary B. Fiedorek, Meg Mundy, Nan Nall, Barbara Owens, Mervyn M. Peskin, M.D., Barbara L. Sand and Laurie Scandurra.

Introduction

TEN YEARS AGO, I graduated with a Bachelor of Music degree in Voice from an excellent school. My musical background was solid, but I was a total innocent when it came to the business of music. I didn't know how to write a résumé, take a good head shot or plan graphic materials for presentation. I didn't even know where to find out about auditions. As you can imagine, the subjects of management and publicity were mystifying. I think my classmates and I thought it would merely be a year or two before we signed our Met contracts. (Ignorance really *is* bliss!)

Well, I've steered through the choppy waters of a professional career and arrived at shore having sung two movie soundtracks, performed with an orchestra throughout Greece, and marketed my own ensemble, which has toured Europe and made numerous appearances in this country.

About a year ago, I held auditions for a new flutist for my trio and heard quite a few talented musicians, graduates of the nation's finest schools. Not one of them had a well-merchandised résumé, not one could present an 8x10 photograph, several wrote awkward cover letters, and one called me at eleven at night to ask me how I was coming with my decision!

"Ah," I thought to myself . . . "I've isolated a problem here. Apparently I'm not the only one who didn't learn these skills in college." The musicians I questioned spoke bitterly about their lack of preparation.

I began to ask my friends to show me their résumés, pictures, and demo cassettes, and we discussed their results. One woman, an outstanding soprano who had been a Met Finalist and a Fulbright scholar, and had performed at the Kennedy Center to rave *Washington Post* reviews, was having a particularly difficult time. She kept receiving form letters turning down her requests for auditions and asking her to get more experience before she applied again! One glance at her résumé and picture told me why. Three pages long, her résumé was chock full of inconsequential information that did nothing but obscure her considerable accomplishments. Her photo was distant and unengaging.

THE POWER OF PERCEPTION

I've always suspected that there is a correlation between appearance and the *perception* of competency. Unfortunately, the materials preceding a young musician often do more to sabotage than to excite. A poor showing in a photo, résumé, brochure, demo cassette or in the area of business savvy can undermine even a great talent.

Today, more than ever, a career in music is a business. We who aspire to the profession must have talent, technique, repertoire, health, *and* the know-how of professional self-promotion. The business is rife with myth and misinformation, and there are few points of reference to guide a young musician. When I scouted the market for books on the necessary nonmusical aspects of a career, I found one that told where to find a women's hotel and (unbelievably) an abortion, but failed to mention how to write a résumé.

Then where could a musician go to find this information? Whenever I asked this question, I received prophetically veiled answers such as "Those who are meant to find out, will," and "These things simply can't be taught—a musician picks them up here and there . . . ."

Well, I didn't agree. I was convinced this knowledge could be articulated plainly and analytically. I began to write down the tips, methods, and how-to's I had painfully picked up "here and there," and I reviewed some of the systems I had worked out. Interviews with other professionals answered many of my questions, and in March of 1983 I began to market a seminar entitled "Managing in the Musical Marketplace."

These seminars revealed that musicians are bright, energetic, and just hungry for facts, focus, and direction. I received quite a few follow-up calls in which people reported that their new confidence about their professional image helped them give more confident auditions. A few musicians felt that their reworked résumé and photo provoked a more enthusiastic response from their auditioners. All the way around, the situation had improved. I decided then to write this book.

WHAT'S IN IT FOR YOU?

The Performing Artist's Handbook can work for you in a number of ways, and I'd like to suggest a few:

First of all, read each chapter and absorb the merchandising techniques given throughout. Then, have what I call a "shake-down" discussion with yourself. What are your strengths? (What are your weaknesses?) What makes you different from all the competition and worth investigating? By all means seek professional evaluation, but ultimately you've got to know yourself. And this takes a lot of time and work.

Once you have some ideas on how you want to present yourself in the musical marketplace, assess your budget and think carefully about where to prune and preen. Remember that if you want to be taken seriously as a professional, everything that represents you must be of professional quality. Your representatives—résumés, photographs, stationery, brochures, demo cassettes—are expensive investments and will each require research and preparation. Work on upgrading your materials a bit at a time.

Now, try experimenting with some of the organizational techniques. The idea is to gauge your results, discard what doesn't work and keep maintaining what does. Your new systems of organization will leave you with more time to learn that new opera score, quartet, or concerto.

Should you decide it's time to make your recital debut, photocopy the Chapter 10 Checklist, transfer your specific dates to it and begin the countdown.

I'd like to say a few things to the musician just beginning the pathway to a professional career. At first you may feel put off by all this talk of marketing. Shouldn't your talent speak for itself? Of course it should. But all the talent in the world won't help if you're not called in for the audition. There's a tremendous amount of competition, and you've got to make sure people recognize your abilities and respond to you confidently. Only then can your talent really speak for itself.

Don't be overwhelmed by the amount of information and projects to pursue. Concentrate instead on buying a good typewriter, a small file cabinet, and professional stationery. This equipment will launch your "business office" and help arrange your systems. Put together a résumé and head shot and don't be ashamed if the résumé is a little on the thin side— wouldn't it be suspect if it weren't? Then, take a good healthy look at the "Quasi-Sherlock Holmes Method of Audition and Job Investigation" listed in Chapter 1. Start typing letters and take every audition you can. Also, investigate workshops, master classes and summer programs. These will all help fill out your résumé and bring you into contact with people. As you'll read in Chapter 11, networking throughout a career is *extremely* important. Read the other chapters to give yourself a taste for the future and to build up your understanding of the requirements that will come with it.

The course of your career will be smoother with guidance to keep you from making wrong turns or following dead ends. The intention of this book is to show you how to present your unique talents clearly and professionally and to help you decipher and contend with the often inscrutable road signs along the way.

Janice Papolos
New York

GETTING STARTED

CHAPTER 1

Managing On Your Own

NOT TOO LONG AGO, I was a soprano auditioning with hundreds of others for all the usual apprenticeship programs and competitions. Waiting to be cast in other people's productions seemed a slow and often demoralizing way to build a career. It soon became apparent that I had to find a way to create a market for my specific talents and that I would not be able to rely on the traditional channels of career building for which a music degree had prepared me.

The idea for our trio took hold when I was asked to perform at my twin sister's outdoor wedding. My mother's dogged refusal to have a piano dragged over her lawn forced me to consider an alternative form of accompaniment. I chose a piece scored for voice, guitar, and flute, and liked the combination so much that I decided there just might be life after opera after all.

Straightaway I began a search for music. I tracked down publishers from California to Spain, hired an arranger to write for the ensemble, studied a few of the offbeat languages in which I would be singing, and got the group into a strenuous rehearsal schedule.

Now the marketing aspects of the group came into high relief and there were major decisions to be made. We all felt that concerts had become starchy affairs, and our aim was to perform our unconventional repertoire with color and drama. Entertainment and accessibility were our bywords. After putting together an expensive brochure, stationery, cards, photographs and demo tapes, we had to begin beating the bushes for jobs in order to build a résumé and gain performance experience. Several people mentioned that dread word *debut*, but to do one correctly would have cost at least five thousand dollars, and the morning after we might have nothing but two well-phrased quotes. It seemed clear that resources should be channeled toward jobs that paid.

PERSEVERANCE PAYS

All of us have to do our share of showcasing to get started, but here we proceeded with caution, pursuing only those appearances that would be of maximum value. For instance, I felt that our program would be appropriate for the United Nations, and that a performance there would "speak internationally," so I began investigating a booking. Two weeks and nearly twenty-four phone calls later, no one had consented to act as sponsor. Discouraged but not defeated, I continued trying different approaches and finally found someone at the U.N. who thought it was a great idea and produced the concert for us. Sometimes it's that twenty-fifth call! Perseverance has also brought us performances in New York in such diverse places as the Citicorp Center, Federal Hall, Rockefeller Center and the Brooklyn Museum. Unlikely as it sounds, we've also done a USO tour which involved twenty concerts in West Germany and Berlin—but that's another, longer story.

After a number of concerts, we reached the stage where publicity became essential, and we were advised to seek a press agent. The cost was prohibitive, so I began searching through the newspaper and weekly magazines to find other avenues of exposure for the group. A call to the editor of a major newspaper's entertainment guide produced a request for some information about an upcoming concert date. He was interested to learn that we were perhaps the only trio of soprano, guitar, and flute on the East Coast (and he especially liked the title of one of our songs, "Father's a Drunkard and Mother Is Dead"), but he informed me that he had forty press releases for that date and could only feature four events. I called again, but he made no promises. Apparently most press agents feel their job is completed with the mailing of the release. Once again, I found that persistence pays—we were featured first in his column that day.

MANAGING YOURSELF

The word *manager* is sometimes all it takes to make some musicians froth at the mouth (and don't we all have our little stories?) but I think there is a tendency to project all of our anxieties onto management and have unrealistic expectations of it. Any conscientious manager will stress that it takes a minimum of three years to work up even a moderate season for most artists. Managers have full rosters and offices to look after, and no one garners total attention. Besides, a manager cannot sell you without such selling points as reviews, some publicity, and a performance history, so you've got to act on your own behalf for a while anyway.

Allen Hughes of the *New York Times*, when writing an article about competition winners, said, "Too many of those names have ended up a little older, maybe even a little wiser, but with next to nothing in the way of performing careers once the prearranged engagements that came with their prizes have been fulfilled." Shocking as this statement may be, it highlights the fact that times have changed and none of us can blithely depend upon competitions, management, etc., to establish ourselves in the business of music. A great many of us must find alternative vehicles for career development. There *are* resources out there, just as there are people who want to experience the joys of music. Innovative ideas need to be pursued to make these connections and to create new audiences.

So where do you begin? Well, I won't tell you that it's easy, but all journeys (and careers) begin with a single step. Listed here are quite a few steps to get you started.

THE QUASI-SHERLOCK HOLMES METHOD OF AUDITION AND JOB INVESTIGATION

- Network! Talk to people—get to know them through workshops, classes, church or synagogue jobs, etc. They can give you leads and let you know what's going on in the business.

- If you feel you are ready, call the doyen or doyenne in your field and ask to play or sing for him or her. Be prepared to pay the hourly fee, but ask for an honest assessment of where you should be going in your career. This is a good way to introduce yourself and get some feedback and direction. If the person you called does not do this sort of thing, ask who might agree to do it.

- Instrumentalists should read the *International Musician* (published monthly by the AF of M), *Das Orchester* (it's in German, but it monthly lists openings in European orchestras and chamber ensembles—available at most music libraries), *Chamber Music Magazine,* and any magazine or newsletter about your particular instrument. Singers should read *Opera News, Back Stage, Show Business,* and Central Opera Service's *Career Guide for the Young American Singer.* These publications list auditions, competitions, workshops, and grants.

● Read the Sunday newspaper's music listings and give a call when you recognize that an organization, church, or opera group repeatedly presents concerts or productions. Ask when they hold auditions and what their working procedures are.

Talk to your state and regional arts councils—they can point you in some good directions. Quite a few councils place young artists on their rosters and promote state and regional tours. Addresses and phone numbers of all state and regional arts councils are given in the appendices.

● Find out whether there are corporations or art galleries or even shopping centers that would sponsor a concert for you. These firms may have functions for which you could also provide entertainment. Speak to the Public Relations Office—the people there are the most likely to be responsive.

● Go and see restaurant and hotel managers or owners about playing Sunday brunches.

● Link up with caterers and send a mailing to all prospective brides to see whether your string quartet or ensemble could help them down the aisle or provide beautiful music after the ceremony.

● Investigate women's clubs and service organizations. Find out if they'll pay you for entertainment at their luncheon meetings.

● Contact libraries and schools with good ideas for special programs.

● Contact museums and find out about their musical programs and concert series.

● Do a mailing and call the heads of concert series. These are listed in the back pages of the *Musical America International Directory of the Performing Arts* (hereafter referred to as the *Musical America Directory*), which is published each December and available in most music stores and libraries. When you call, ask about their procedures for hiring—do they need a tape, what other materials would they want to see, etc.

- Read the back pages of the *Musical America Directory* for a comprehensive listing of competitions and contests—write for particulars and decide which ones you wish to enter.

- Advertise yourself—in magazines and newspapers; for parties, soirées, and functions.

- If you're marketing an ensemble, investigate the advantages of becoming a not-for-profit corporation so that you can attract grants and contributions and establish a concert series for yourself. Take a look at the "Notes on Not-For-Profit" section in the Appendices.

  Then, spend some time at the Foundation Center Library Collection nearest you and research foundation grants. Write to local government officials, congressmen/women and senators and ask them to give you information about government grants (their research assistants will be able to provide the most current information on the subject). See the Appendices of this book for Foundation Center locations and more detailed information on government grants.

- Find out if you qualify to participate in the Affiliate Artists or Young Audiences programs. The experience is wonderful and you are rather steadily employed. Affiliate Artists has placed solo performers in more than a thousand communities in forty-six states, Washington, D.C., Puerto Rico, and Canada. At the heart of the program is the concept of the "Informance," an informal, informational performance combining artistic repertory with a lively dialogue between performer and audience. The residencies vary in length from one to six weeks. To find out more about the program contact:

  Affiliate Artists, Inc.
  155 W. 68th St.
  New York NY 10023
  (212)580-2000

Young Audiences was established thirty years ago to provide educational programs in the performing arts for school children. More than twenty-five Chapter Service Centers around the country audition and employ individual and ensemble performers to present performances, demonstrations, workshops, and residencies. If you can indicate a capacity to communicate effectively with children and you wish to see if there's a chapter in your state, call or write the national office:

> Young Audiences
> 115 E. 92nd St.
> New York NY 10028
> (212)831-8110

- Keep up with what's happening in your town or city—where would an artist be needed for a special celebration? For instance, there were many performances during the Brooklyn Bridge Centennial—lots of work opportunities.

- Contact the entertainment offices of the major shipping lines. (Check the Sunday Travel Section of the *New York Times* to collect their names and phone numbers.) Find out if you can be hired for a cruise; it's a great way to work and vacation at the same time.

- For those who have a special gift for teaching, establish a studio and advertise for students. If you're interested in teaching on the university level, read the *College Music Society*. It monthly lists teaching positions across the United States and it's available through the University of Colorado, Regent Box 44, Boulder CO 80309.

  Also, the Lutton Music Personnel Service matches musicians to university, conservatory, public, and private schools, and church music positions. In existence since 1913, they are the only music personnel agency in the country. Write them at the following address for particulars:

> The Lutton Music Personnel Agency
> Box 13985
> Gainesville FL 32604
> (904)376-9055

- One more. I advise you to get in touch with the National Guild of Community Schools of the Arts, Inc., P.O. Box 583, Teaneck NJ 07666; (201)836-5594. They publish a national guide of non-degree-granting music schools, and you can investigate the possibility of becoming a performing faculty member at one of the schools in your area. Pressure-sensitive address labels are available by region for a small fee.

ETUDES FOR AUDITIONING

As you can see, you've got your work cut out for you! But before you get busy investigating the audition circuit, let me review the process and point out a few things that will ensure better results and a happier time.

Auditions are a fact of professional life. I used to think that once you had management your auditioning days were over and you would be hired on the strength of your manager's raves. Not so. Until you become an acknowledged international star, people will want to hear you and decide for themselves. The situation may become more cordial and personal—it will still be an audition.

Now, no one is going to argue with you if even the *thought* of an audition makes your heart pound or your palms sweat. There are so many anxiety-producing factors at play. Who are these people who will judge you and say yes or no to your greatest desires? What do they want? How should you act? What will happen?

It's extremely difficult to have to perform in an unfamiliar, tense, and judgmental atmosphere, and anxiety would be a natural reaction. A certain amount of excitement can be channeled into a more brilliant and alert performance. The problems begin when the anxiety becomes overwhelming. But this won't happen if you're prepared, focused, and realize that there's only one thing you're supposed to do at an audition—display your talent as quickly and clearly as possible. As you take more and more auditions, you'll learn about yourself and the situations, and the difficulties *will* diminish. Let me help you get started.

First of all, prepare good strong audition material—pieces that show off your skills in the best, most exciting light. Then, decide which auditions and competitions you'd like to take or enter, and call to find out about application and deadline requirements. Request a time slot as soon as possible as they fill up quickly and you may get closed out. Read Chapters 2 and 3 in order to prepare your résumé and head shot, and take a look at Chapter 4 so you'll know how to write for and confirm auditions as well as how to dress for them.

Once you've got your date and time slot, check through the following list of advice, do's, and don'ts:

1. If you're coming in for the audition from a distance, find out if there's a warm-up room you can use. Just give a call and ask. If no such facilities exist on the premises, find out if you can rent a re-

hearsal studio nearby or if a friend will let you use his house or apartment. If your only option is the bathroom, be considerate!

2. If possible, find out for whom you will be auditioning and in what kind of room. This knowledge will make the experience more personal and human and thus less frightening.

3. If you have the choice of bringing your own accompanist or using the staff accompanist supplied by the auditioners, *bring your own!* You'll be well-rehearsed and make a much better impression. Plus, you won't have to make frantic whispered tempi comments to the stranger on the piano bench. If you *must* use the pianist provided, work out before the audition the quickest, clearest way to indicate your musical needs and choices and mark the repeats or cuts clearly in the music you hand him. If the pianist does fumble and things go badly, don't glare, make caustic remarks or snap your fingers to demonstrate tempi. It's degrading to the pianist and it makes you look terrible. You took a chance, you lost—handle it gracefully. Besides, the pianist may have a vote.

4. Have your music organized so that you can turn to the selections immediately. Fumbling through scores ruins your composure and makes you look unprepared. If you're using photocopied music, make sure it is taped together in an accordion fashion so that it can be spread out at the piano or on your music stand. There are often drafts or air conditioners and flying photocopies present a real problem. While we're speaking of photocopying . . . I recently heard of a young musician who was disqualified in a competition for using photocopied music still protected under copyright law. A word to the wise . . .

5. Bring along at least two sets of your résumé and head shot. This way, a committee can tune into you quickly. If your résumé looks good and is clear to read, you may get a more attentive response.

6. *Get There Early!* You'll need to unbundle, relax, and warm up your instruments, hands, etc. If the schedule is running ahead, the auditioners will appreciate being able to hear you sooner and they'll notice your professionalism.

7. So that nondiscriminating hiring policies can be maintained, many orchestral auditions will take place behind a screen. This means that an instrumentalist is given a number and brought to a screened-off area to play for judges whose decisions cannot be bi-

ased by race or gender factors. Therefore, the tap-tap-tap of high heels would definitely defy the logistical design here . . . women, wear flats!

Playing behind a screen may strike you as inhuman and isolating. However, it does promote fairness to all; and think of it this way—you don't have to be charming or chipper, you can remain focused and put your best into the music.

8. If the circumstances seem friendly and you are rather close to the auditioners, introduce yourself *and* your accompanist. Be natural and warm but not overfamiliar. Your job is not to ingratiate, but to show what you can do.

9. Don't look disappointed if the judges don't pick your favorite piece. Also, be prepared if the auditioners ask you to pick the first selection and don't hem and haw. Never offer anything you don't really want to play or sing.

10. Don't be upset if you are stopped in the middle of the piece—it can and does happen and not necessarily for negative reasons. There may not be time for more, or the judges may be totally convinced of your worthiness and may not need to hear anymore. Try not to personalize it. If the person before you got to perform two pieces and after your *one* you hear, "Thank you," don't ask if you can play or sing something else. In this case your persistence will be resented.

11. If you're not well, don't try to brave out an audition. Cancel it. If you go and do poorly, you will never erase this first impression. Reschedule or wait until the next set of auditions. Besides, if you're ill and insist on carrying on, you look too desperate. *And,* there's too much temptation to cough, sniff, or otherwise display your infirmities. Get healthy and go wow them the next time!

12. If you're a singer auditioning with an aria, find out if the judges would like to see it as a piece of acting or whether they would be more comfortable if you stood straight and sang. I've had stage directors ask me to really "use the stage," but I know of one woman whose request to use a chair on the stage met with shocked disapproval.

It's also a good idea to find out which operas are being planned for the next few seasons and try to sing something which demonstrates your suitability for a role. However, if you find that the company is doing *La Bohème* and you announce you'd like to sing "Musetta's Waltz," you may hear groans or laughter from the panel. (Hours and hours of that aria could drive anyone crazy!) Ask them first if they'd like to hear that or some other Puccini selection.

13. Try to keep your energy up but don't do any Marlon Brando-style emoting exercises. You'll look unstable and be finished before you begin.

14. Do not editorialize on your performance with grimaces or muttered curses as you leave. You probably did better than you realize, but the auditioners will be put off by your unprofessional response. Smile, say thank you, and leave graciously. And remember, your audition is not over until you are outside the building. Don't pass through the waiting area breathing horror stories and rolling your eyes. Also, don't do a hatchet job on the staff accompanist. You will make the people waiting even more nervous and it's not fair.

15. You'll soon begin to recognize a lot of the same faces in the audition waiting areas. Help each other through. This is an excellent opportunity for networking and you can give and gain some valuable support.

If you don't do a good audition, the world won't stop. On the other hand, if you do a great audition, the world won't stop either. Keep some perspective on the subject and use auditions to learn about yourself. There are many steps on the pathway to a professional career, and rarely do things get rolling immediately. While you play the waiting game, don't get caught between the poles of bitterness and blame. Keep working and get ready for the next . . . "NEXT!"

CHAPTER 2

The Art of the Résumé

WHEN I FIRST CAME TO NEW YORK, I worked in a designers' showroom to support my lessons and life. One afternoon, the receptionist told me to pick up on extension 1031. I did, and the person at the other end identified himself as a Broadway casting agent! He requested that I show up the next day to audition for a revival of *The King and I* and I got so nervous that I could barely hear what he was saying. He calmly repeated the time and address and reminded me to bring a résumé and head shot.

I turn red with embarrassment when I think of what I handed the show's director the next day. But I was sure it was only my talent that mattered. *Mistake number one.* In this instance they were kind about it (at least to my face), but not long afterward I saw an agent at a well-known firm. He took one look at my three-page résumé and photo and began to circle around me like a vulture. "What kind of résumé is this?" he sneered. "I won't read it; you're wasting my time." I made some joke in agreement that perhaps less really was more, and sank lower in my seat.

Then, he gestured at my hair and said, "What's this with the frizz? Your picture says your hair is straight." Explaining the cause and effect of a permanent wave seemed a useless appeasement. After a short, painful conversation, I stood up and let him know I didn't think either of us was looking for what the other had to offer. I left.

Looking back now, was he insufferable and rude and was his behavior inexcusable? Yes. Was he right about the résumé and head shot? I grudgingly have to admit, yes. This leads us into the subject and purpose of the résumé.

Your résumé should be a *single* sheet of paper that lists your name, address, telephone number, instrument or voice category, union affiliations, physical description, work experience, training, and special skills. It is not your autobiography.

The one thing I got right at that humiliating interview was that less really is more. Cramming a lot of information onto the résumé is confusing and only makes you appear to be scraping the bottom of the barrel. Directors and auditioners leaf through hundreds of résumés; and they must be able to see your most important credentials in one uncomplicated glance. The time for details is when they're interested in hiring you. As a matter of fact, the more white space on the page, the less discouraging it looks and the greater the chances it will be read.

You've got to imagine a busy person in an office—the desk is cluttered with résumés and photos, the phone is ringing off the hook and there are deadlines all around. If your résumé enters this situation and looks unattractive or seems like a chore to read, it will lie around until it can be comfortably "misplaced."

Your bid for attention may net you a twenty-second glance. Make sure it tunes the reader in and makes an immediate impact.

Briefly, your résumé is a skeletal outline designed to give practical information and pique future interest. Remember, when you get longer in experience your résumé gets shorter and more selective.

Please study the sample résumés on the following pages. Notice how quickly you get a sense of the professional level of these artists you've not met.

ANY QUESTIONS?

Here are some of the most frequently asked questions about résumés:

"How come I have to put 'call collect' next to my out-of-town number?"

About once a month, the director of a musical organization receives the telephone bill. Depending on his degree of excitability, he may *threaten* the staff to cut down on long-distance calls, thus cutting *you* from the picture. Don't give them the excuse—urge them to call you collect, and if you meet them, make them understand that you will be happy to travel to any audition or job.

Jody Rapport

Lyric Soprano

AEA-AGMA

2 Howard Street
Largo, Vermont 05301
(802)556-0132 (call collect)

Height: 5'5½"
Weight: 130 lbs.
Hair: Chestnut
Eyes: Brown

OPERA

La Traviata	Violetta	
Die Fledermaus	Rosalinda	Purchase Opera Theatre
La Bohème	Mimi	
Pagliacci	Nedda	
The Dialogues of the Carmelites	Blanche	Purchase Opera Theatre
L'Amico Fritz	Suzel	Opera Theatre of Northern Virginia
Susannah	Susannah	
Rita	Rita	Baltimore Opera Touring Theatre
La Voix Humaine	Woman	

SOLO ORCHESTRAL ENGAGEMENTS/AWARDS

Ravel's Schéhérazade   The National Symphony at the Kennedy Center
(M. Rostropovich-Music Director)

"...Jody Rapport, a glorious soprano of great promise."
—Paul Hume, the Washington Post

1984 Regional Finalist—Metropolitan Opera Auditions
1983 Winner—Sarah Caldwell Boston Opera Auditions
1983 Regional Finalist—Metropolitan Opera Auditions
1982 Fulbright Scholar—Stuttgart, West Germany
1981 Finalist—Luciano Pavarotti International Voice Competition

TRAINING

Oberlin Conservatory—B. Music
Voice: Margaret Harshaw, Nan Nall, Richard Miller
Opera: Barbara Owens, Ernst Poettgen, Henry Butler
Master Classes: Alberta Masiello, Martin Katz, John Wustman

SPECIAL SKILLS
Southern and English dialects, Chess (winner of U.S. Junior Open Chess Tournament—Women's Division), Tennis

ROSA LAMOREAUX

Lyric Soprano

2067 Broadway
Suite 27
New York, NY 10023
(212) 799-9099 (service)

Height: 5'5"
Weight: 135 lbs.
Hair: Ash Blonde
Eyes: Hazel

OPERA

Giulio Cesare	Cleopatra
Le Nozze de Figaro	Susanna
Don Giovanni	Zerlina
Cosi fan Tutte	Despina

ROLES STUDIED

Die Zauberflote	Pamina
Pelléas et Mélisande	Mélisande
Gianni Schicchi	Lauretta
The Medium	Monica

SOLO ENGAGEMENTS/ ORATORIO & ORCHESTRAL

United States Tour, Roger Wagner Chorale
Washington Bach Consort, The Messiah
William Hall Chorale, The Messiah

BACH PERFORMANCES

Coffee Cantata	*At the Kennedy Center*
B Minor Mass	*Bethlehem Bach Festival*
Magnificat in D, Christmas Oratorio	
St. Matthew Passion	
Cantatas: 140, 57, 51, 84, 115, 205	

AWARDS/REVIEWS

1983 Finalist, Oratorio Society of New York Competition
1983 Fellowship, Bach Aria Festival at Stony Brook
1982 Winner of Vocal Competition, Aspen Music Festival

"1st class singing by Rosa Lamoreaux ... the prime highlight in a program of highlights."
THE WASHINGTON POST

"Rosa Lamoreaux gave a stunningly beautiful performance as Cleopatra."
SUN TELEGRAM, San Bernardino, CA.

EDUCATION

Bachelor of Music, Master of Music. University of Redlands, CA.
Associate of Royal College of Music. London, England.
Voice : Richard Barrett, Lila Stuart, Larra Browning-Henderson
Master Classes: Jon Humphrey, Phyllis Bryn-Julson
Jan De Gaetani, Joan Dornemann

Marc Stocker

Flute/Piccolo

21 Stowell Drive
Presto, Arizona 85252
(602)561-4284
(answering machine)

Height: 5'11"
Weight: 145 lbs.
Hair: Lt. Brown
Eyes: Brown

ORCHESTRAL ENGAGEMENTS

Colorado Philharmonic Orchestra (solo piccolo/asst. principal flute)
Phoenix Symphony Orchestra
National Orchestra of New York
Juilliard Orchestra
Brooklyn Lyric Opera

CHAMBER MUSIC ENSEMBLES

Colorado Philharmonic Woodwind Quintet
The Atlantic Flute Trio (flute, violin, cello)
The Runners Jazz Quintet (as bassist and manager)

RECITALS

Avery Fisher Hall, New York City (w. Jean-Pierre Rampal & Julius Baker)
Alice Tully Hall, New York City

AWARDS

1983 Arthur Ross Scholarship in flute—Juilliard School, Full Tuition
1982 Cornelius Crane Fund Scholarship—Juilliard School

EDUCATION

Juilliard School of Music (M.M. to be awarded 1984), Oberlin Conservatory
Teachers: Julius Baker (New York Philharmonic, Princ. Flute)
          Samuel Baron (Bach Aria Group)
          James Walker (Los Angeles Philharmonic, Co-princ. Flute)

SPECIAL SKILLS
Bassist, Arranger, Cyclist, Carpenter

Also, if you have an answering machine or service put it in parentheses after the phone number. It's a comfort to the casting person to know the message can be conveyed to you with only one call. It will make them *make* that call faster.

"What are the rules or guidelines when listing physical characteristics?"

Your height should be how tall (or small) you stand in bare feet. Don't lie about your weight—if you feel the urge, it's a sure sign you need a diet. When you list your hair and eye color, be creative so as to be more memorable. Nothing is so boring as to read brown hair/brown eyes over and over again. Doesn't chestnut/sienna/auburn hair and dark brown eyes sound more intriguing? I admit this advice applies more to female musicians. We can't all have blonde, green-eyed statistics but we don't have to fade into the woodwork either!

Note! Instrumentalists have the option of omitting the physical characteristics.

"What about giving dates?"

Don't. Dates of birth, productions, etc. are superfluous and can work against you. The only date of interest is the year you won a big contest. A "for instance" that supports this: I was doing some casting for Universal Pictures and we had a very talented young actor in the office. He seemed rather withdrawn and depressed and later, looking over his résumé (which was covered with dates) we all noticed that the professional activity stopped in 1981. Everyone of us ventured an opinion as to why there was a two-year gap in the work schedule and what stuck in our minds was the possibility that he'd had a nervous breakdown and been hospitalized! We were nervous about taking a chance with him.

The next day, I was putting some things on the desk when I came across the résumé again, and, by *accident*, saw that there was a second page attached with the dates continuing impressively up to the present! So much for idle speculation; but this should underscore two points—the résumé should be one page only, and all the dates except for prize-winning years should be left in your memory.

"What's the best way to organize a résumé?"

Your résumé should be set up like a menu—meat/fish/poultry—make the categories clear.

Merchandise yourself for the position. If you are applying for a job in opera, the résumé should list those credits first. If you are an instrumentalist auditioning for an ensemble, list your chamber music experience before your orchestra credits. You will probably need two or three versions of your performing résumé to cover the different kinds of audition possibilities.

Singers! If you need to make money in stock this summer, you would do better to emphasize your musicals and dramatic experience and go lightly on the operatic credits.

The other question that confronts the singer is the matter of listing operatic and musical credits on the same page. I try not to be rigid about this, but it often confuses the auditioner to read from opera to Broadway. He'll want to know what the talent is really right for. It's best to leave out the musicals unless you have too few credits or you've starred on Broadway and, if you dance or act, list it under "Training" or "Special Skills."

"In what order should I list my operatic roles?"

Because we're trying to merchandise you as a lead singer (and therefore a moneymaker), you would be wise to list your most impressive, bread-and-butter roles first and list the more obscure, smaller roles further down.

"How much information should I list for each credit?"

If you have performed a role or played a concert in a prestigious place, appeared with a well-known artist or have been conducted by a famous conductor, list it as a second or third column on the sheet. Otherwise just list the work and the role or the concerto and orchestra. Try not to stress university or amateur auspices. This information levels the professional impression and distracts the reader. For example, let them concentrate on the fact that you *can* sing a Violetta. Also, if you had a chorus part in a production and there was a name to the role, list it; it looks better. If you were the understudy be sure to note it. If you understudied and got to perform the role once, your résumé should list that role.

"What's the reason for listing special skills?"

There are several. Professionally, you might land a job because you have some athletic skill, speak a language or dialect or play another instrument. For singers, the ability to play an instrument signals competency as a musician. On a more personal level, you reveal here in just a few words your interests and the kind of person you are. This might just strike a chord with the decision maker. After all, an interesting, three-dimensional person is an asset to any organization. Let them see your humanity.

Some final notes: If you have some extremely impressive credits, please don't dilute their impact by listing unprofessional ones. Let it be short, it will speak volumes. For those who sing in church or synagogue, I hope the money is good, but the job doesn't belong on the résumé. However, if you can persuade the organization to sponsor a concert for you, definitely list that under recitals. In the beginning, you must think carefully about every job you take. Can it be used on my résumé, or is the money what I need? If the job doesn't serve one or the other (your résumé or pocketbook), channel your energies toward a more marketable you.

Also! When listing teachers or schools pick the three most impressive. The mind can't gather in more than this amount and the longer the list, the less effective the impact. You have a choice of labeling this category as *Education* or *Training*. Some people feel *Education* is too academic and *Training* sounds more professional, but that is solely personal taste.

FINAL PRODUCTION

- Have your résumé typed by a professional if typing is not your forte. It looks *so much better.* Also, there are businesses that will put your résumé on a floppy disc so it's a simple matter to add, delete, or rearrange information. Check trade papers for their names and addresses.

- Staple the résumé (cut down to 8x10 size) back to back with your photo, on all four corners. The bands of the staples should be visible on the picture side, the little teeth on the résumé side. Your photo looks better this way. Remember to staple tightly—draw blood and you won't be liked. Don't glue the photo and résumé because glue stains, ripples, and you can't pull the pages apart when you want to update the résumé or photo. A staple remover would do nicely should you wish to make a change.

Important! Your name and union affiliations and category titles can all be in uppercase letters, but to increase legibility, everything else should be upper *and* lower case. (See Chapter 6.) It's an advantage to have your name in a bold logotype so that it really stands out. (See Chapter 4.) If you've had professional stationery designed your logo can be reduced and pasted up on the résumé original.

I would recommend using a quality paper stock of 20 percent rag bond. I once leafed through a lot of business résumés sent to a prestigious firm. The Harvard and Yale applicants used a fine, grained stock that made a more dignified impression. However, I wouldn't suggest typesetting or offset printing because you'll add and update so frequently. Some of today's photocopy equipment is so good that you'll be able to have your résumés photocopied.

As often as you need to update your résumé, do so. Remember to take off a lesser credit to add the more impressive one. Use your new résumé as a good excuse to contact someone you have performed for in the past, or hope to work with in the future. You can circle the change in red to signal your addition and write a personal cover letter that implies you are working, progressing, gathering steam, and ready for more work. The idea is to keep your name and credits in front of as many people as often as possible and every résumé (or photo) update is a good and relevant excuse to do so.

CHAPTER 3

The A-to-Zs of 8x10s

I WAS SITTING IN MY wing chair on a Thursday evening, thoroughly discouraged about the rough times I was having in the music business. My session of self-pity was interrupted by the telephone. It was *Newsweek* magazine offering to buy an article I'd submitted about my ensemble's European tour. They wanted to set up a photo session at my home the next day! Immediately my world shrank to a one-inch-by-one-inch space (the size of the published photo) and I was caught out by my lack of knowledge in preparing for a good one. It was too late to get a makeup artist or consult on hair, wardrobe, or jewelry. I was on my own. The next day during the session, standing against the blank wall in my kitchen I agonized over every choice I'd frantically made. Phooey on that! I survived, the photo was fine, and here are the *facts:*

First of all, artists need black-and-white photographs (normally 8x10 in size) throughout a career. They'll be required for publicity purposes, brochures and graphic materials, and, right from the start, as the complement to a résumé. In this instance, the photo or head shot will introduce you physically and jog the memory of the auditioner when you're not around.

There was a time when an intense, "artistic" shot was in vogue. No more. The classical field has begun to keep pace with the more commercial aspects of the music business and the personality and humor of an artist has become important. Your picture should make a single, strong impression and connect you humanly with the decision maker or audience. Don't turn people off because your mien seems formidable, indifferent, or snooty.

Before I push on, I want to tell you a little confidence shared by a director I knew. One dreary afternoon, he and the production staff were poring over résumés and photos, trying to find someone right for a role. They had had some difficult personalities in the office that morning and weren't up for any more trouble. Eventually, they came across a natural, friendly-looking photo of a girl and the director turned and said, "Call her in, maybe she'll cheer us up." The message? Never forget that you are a human being trying to catch the attention of human beings who have human feelings and responses.

Now let's get more specific. The photo should look like you, but, for our purposes, a groomed version of you. If you are a woman, by all means have your hair done by a professional and hire a makeup artist to *naturally* bring out your eyes and cheekbones and outline your mouth. (Often one person can do your hair and makeup—ask your photographer to recommend someone.) Men should make sure their hair and/or beards are trimmed. The better you look, the more confident you'll feel in front of the camera.

What are we aiming for? A picture that conveys energy, a dynamic, *breathing* person, someone we'd like to know better. It can be sensual without overkill, but a twinkle in the eye and a feeling of warmth are what make you interesting.

Good pictures always seem to convey an attitude. The person really is thinking something and it's definitely *not* "cheese." The eyes and mouth are in it together, so to speak, and a certain charge comes across. I like it when an artist shows a lit-up enthusiasm or a sense of humor. People who have a small smirk in the mouth and a slightly raised eyebrow and seem to be saying, "I've got something *very* interesting to tell you" are intriguing. When a strong quality or attitude is present, it grabs the attention of the viewer and provokes a response.

So when you're having your pictures taken, think of situations, scenes, people, or even pets—anything that will inspire real feeling, warmth, or humor.

An instrumentalist should include the instrument in the picture in a creative way, so give it a lot of thought. Large instruments or pianos present more of a problem but notice how the head shot of Panayis Lyras managed to include one. Look through the *Musical America Directory* and keep an eye on flyers in concert halls to get some ideas.

One series of shots should probably be in concert attire, another in something more informal. If you don't experiment, you won't have a choice. An ensemble requires even more imagination and clothing coordination. The photographer of my trio trooped us off to the Brooklyn Bridge and shot us performing against the Manhattan skyline. This is, of course, individual taste, but don't be limited because you didn't think it through.

Before choosing a photographer, talk to people and get recommendations. Then go to the photographers' studios and look at their portfolios. If you like the work, determine how you feel about him or her. Do you feel demeaned or out of sync with the person? If so, you probably won't get good pictures. If you are comfortable with the photographer and think that you might even have fun, you're halfway home. Not every photographer is right for every person. Trust your instincts. Also, you must be very sure of the look you want and communicate it to the photographer. Bring along the pictures in this book or earmark some you like in the *Musical America Directory*. Some perfectly wonderful commercial photographers may not understand the needs of the classical musician, but if *you* know, you'll get what you want.

STEPS TO A FLATTERING PHOTO

Here are some general guidelines for putting your best face forward.

☑ Your eyes should be looking straight into the lens—they are your most important feature. Looking off into the sunset doesn't engage anyone; in fact, it encourages people to follow suit and look away. Note: This statement doesn't always apply to ensembles. A group photo must convey a unity of composition, energy, enthusiasm, and relationship.

☑ Keep jewelry to a minimum, so that nothing gets in the way or grabs attention away from you, and please, no religious jewelry.

☑ Clothing should take no attention away from the face! No busy plaids, stripes, or prints. A simple V-neck looks best on most women since a round neck tends to accentuate a round face. Turtlenecks *can* make you look like a turtle; on the other hand, some men look devastating in them. Solid colors look best. I personally feel that in a photograph, more people look better in black. At any rate, bring two or three changes to your session. Know what you want the outfit to accomplish—a formal, casual, or commercial impression. You'll need different kinds of pictures, so coordinate the looks you want to present. Try *not* to bring more than two or three changes because you'll need time to settle into each outfit in front of the camera, and if you do too much running around you'll get messed up and harried. Remember to think in black-and-white terms and keep in mind that the aqua silk blouse that does so much for your eyes in person will photograph a gray tonality.

☑ Women, don't forget to bring combs, barrettes, and brushes so you can experiment with different hair styles. Also, Blistex helps moisten your lips so your smile doesn't get stuck, and powder from a compact will cover shiny noses, chins, and foreheads.

☑ Lay out all your clothes and accessories the night before and get a good night's sleep. If you have a morning photo session, get up several hours earlier so the puffiness drains out of your face. Don't rush or participate in a crisis. It will undermine your concentration and relaxation.

Most quality photographers will take approximately one hundred shots. Some like to shoot outdoors because natural light is always more flattering (fewer shadows) and it definitely adds a different dimension. A few days after the session, the photographer will present you with the contact sheets, often marking off in red those shots he feels will represent you best. He will probably indicate cropping instructions also. Out of these, you'll choose at least two contrasting shots. If you see others you think may be useful, ask for the additional prices. The photographer will enlarge your choices to 8x10 size and perhaps do a bit of retouching. (Keep it to a minimum; we're after a natural look.)

THE WELL-TEMPERED PHOTOGRAPH

Once you have the 8x10s, go to the best photocopy office you can find. They will make copy negatives and print up the duplications. For the photos which will be coupled with your résumé, it's important to have your name stripped into the bottom of the picture. This will help people put the face with the name and, in case your photo and résumé lose each other, their reunion can take place. Of course, if the photo is for publicity purposes, you'll need to identify the image on the back only (see below). I believe most copy offices duplicate in batches of twenty-five or fifty.

You should also discuss with your photographer and copy person whether the photo should be bordered or bled, glossy or matte finish. I like a matte finish because the high reflectivity of the glossy bothers my eyes and seems less elegant. Newspaper and magazine editors still seem to prefer their results with glossies. You may need some of each finish.

Before I close this chapter, let me mention a few important points, most of which concern the mailing of your photographs:

1. Be sure you have a supply of cardboard to back up and front the photo so it doesn't get bent out of shape.

2. If the photo is going solo (without the résumé), don't identify it on the back by stamping or printing with a pen or pencil—this will show through and render the picture useless for publicity reproduction. Instead, type out a pressure-sensitive label with the name of the artist or ensemble, address and telephone number, and the name of the photographer (for a photo credit) and affix it. Also, never clip anything to a photo. A clip will crack the emulsion and its imprint will appear when the picture is reproduced. Watch those fingerprints!

3. Mark the outside mailing envelope on both sides "PHOTOS—DO NOT BEND!" I can't tell you how many photos come to me marked only "First Class" and are handed to me by the mailman rolled up and tied with string, or stuffed into my mailbox.

And finally . . . remember my permanent frizz fiasco in Chapter 2? If you contemplate any change in hair style or beard growing or shaving, you'll have to get new pictures. Your photo should look as you do *now!* While we're on this subject . . . we are, all of us, growing older by the minute. While a youthful appearance is desired, a photo that makes you appear twenty-six when you're actually forty-five is not appropriate. People tend to silently snicker at your fears or vanity when they meet you in person. Artists who know who they are and what they have to offer earn more respect all the way around.

Panayis Lyras, Piano

Stephanie Chase, Violin

Empire Brass Quintet

Doreen Defeis, Soprano

Grayson Hirst, Tenor

The Galliard Quintet

CHAPTER 4

Professional Polish—Correspondence, Conversation, and Appearance

WE SEE OURSELVES AS ACTIVE performing artists and tend not to think of ourselves as secretaries, typists, administrators, public relations people, merchandisers, or guy/gal Fridays. Let me state this bluntly—you can't be one without being *all* of the others! Honestly, there are days I feel I should change hats as I run from one job to the other. It's a fact of life, though. You are a business, so it's important to know how to create and stock an office from which to work. Then you've got to know how to keep things running smoothly and efficiently, all the while building good will, making connections, and presenting your professional image with panache.

I am going to assume that some people reading this know as little as I did when I started. So, we'll start at the beginning.

The first step toward a professional career is to go to auditions, as many as you can. This means writing to the companies, orchestras, and other potential employers to secure and then confirm the appointments. Later you'll be contacting agents and presenters. This means it's vital, right off, to get a supply of professional stationery and envelopes. These are easy to design yourself, and any competent printer can execute the job. Your name, address, and telephone number should be on the stationery and your name and address on the envelopes. Why? Because something as simple as a request for an audition can register your name in the mind of the decision maker. The publicity is free and it leaves an impression of you as a polished professional. It's the power of the subliminal message. I've met people who don't remember seeing my stationery but remark, "Oh, yes, I've heard of you!" They feel confident about you; you feel good. Get the stationery.

Your professional stationery should be simple and striking. Your name in print, your graphic logo, should make a bold, solid impression. (This means you avoid musical notes, cherubs with trumpets, or pianos.) Your printer should have a selection of readable, distinctive type faces. One color ink on a fine twenty-pound stock will serve you well. The stock can be white, cream, gray, or (Tiffany's would shudder) branch out and try other colors, but make sure they don't obscure legibility. Also, make sure you can purchase a correction fluid that matches so you can correct mistakes. White stock is still the easiest to deal with in the typo department. Standard business size is 8½x11, used with a number 10 envelope.

I remember my first business letter. I got through it with the help of a book and then proceeded to fold it all up in four! Of course, the accepted way is to fold in thirds—the bottom third inward, the top third over to the crease. Fold carefully or risk looking sloppy and indifferent. Then insert the letter in the envelope with the salutation (greeting) facing the flap of the envelope. This way, the reader opens the envelope, pulls out your letter and unfolds it for an immediate reading with your name blazoned across the page.

Keep this format in mind when you design your stationery so that a letter can lie comfortably on your stock without being cramped by fancy graphics. A friend of mine had a very attractive stationery with the logo and address printed diagonally, on the top left and the bottom right. Fitting a letter within its confines required prayer and resulted in curses and crumpled balls of paper.

A letter should be aesthetically pleasing and you must pay attention to placement, margins, and balance. I'm from the prayer school myself, but how I wish I'd been trained to center. These aesthetics apply to the addressing of the mailing envelope also. Your professional image is at stake with everything that bears your name. So do it neatly and tastefully—it *does* matter.

Barbara Solomon

30 October 1983

Dr. Charles Micarelli
Orlando Opera
1900 N. Mills Avenue
Suite 4
Orlando, Florida 32803

Dear Dr. Micarelli:

I spoke with your assistant Nancy yesterday and she asked me to send you my picture and résumé. I would like to sing for you when you come to New York to audition.

Nancy told me that you would be sending out audition times and dates in a few weeks and I look forward to hearing from you.

In the meantime, should you have any questions, please don't hesitate to call me at the number listed below. Thank you for your time.

Sincerely,

Barbara Solomon

Barbara Solomon

10 Warwick Road   Alla Breve, New York 13617   (518) 352-0810

Barbara Solomon

21 November 1983

Dr. Charles Micarelli
Orlando Opera
1900 N. Mills Avenue
Suite 4
Orlando, Florida 32803

Dear Dr. Micarelli:

Thank you for responding to my letter of October 30th. I'm looking forward to singing for you on Monday, the 19th of December at 10:30 a.m. at Studio 58 in the Wellington Hotel.

Although you have my picture and résumé, I'll bring along a fresh set. I'll also plan to bring my accompanist that morning.

Until the 19th, then. Thank you for your interest.

Sincerely,

Barbara Solomon

Barbara Solomon

FUNDAMENTALS

☑ Be sure to call a firm and get the name of the person to whom your letter should be addressed. Just ask the receptionist to direct you by giving her a brief outline of your request. A Dear Sir/Madame is unacceptable and a turn-off. Don't hang up before you check the spelling of the name and firm!

☑ Use a new typewriter ribbon and keep the keys clean so that there are no faint or fuzzy letters.

☑ If you make a typo that can't be fixed accurately or make a mistake in grammar or spelling, redo the letter. Remember, it is speaking for you and will no doubt be kept on file and referred to again.

☑ If you find you need two pages for your communication (this should rarely happen), the second sheet should not bear your logo, but be matching, blank stock. Remember to order these second sheets from the stationer when you place your order.

☑ Always keep copies of your letters on file for future reference.

WRITE IT RIGHT!

A business letter should be brief, relevant, create interest, and reveal your personality. You should state clearly what it is you offer, what it is you want, and what action you would like the reader to take. Don't be over-familiar, but strike a tone that's warm, enthusiastic, and convincing. Try to be imaginative within the parameters of good taste. A "nice" letter from a "nice" person is only that, so strive to be more memorable.

Here are two examples of well-written business letters. One is a bit unusual and will need some additional explanation. The other is a more standard invitation to a manager, concert presenter, or critic.

TELEPHONE TECHNIQUES

There's no getting around it—most of your professional contacts will be established over the telephone. Over the years, I've experimented in order to gauge results. Should I call first, then write as follow-up? Or write and then phone? For those who tend to tighten up when a receiver gets within ten inches of their ear, the following recipe should smooth over some of the rough edges:

Cameron Taylor

14 March 1983

Mr. William Sadler
William Sadler Agency
255 W. 57 Street
New York, New York 10019

Dear Mr. Sadler:

No doubt, by now you've seen the film *Tootsie*. In it, a talented actor turns himself inside-out, upside-down and finally becomes a woman to land a part.

I can't do it! I'm already a woman! I have credentials and talent, I have persistence and stamina and I have frustration to boot!!!

I understand that you have the awesome problems of running an office and building the careers of clients who are constantly projecting their anxieties onto you. So, you can call me honey, you can call me sweetie, you can call me Tootsie . . . JUST CALL ME!

Warmest regards,

Cameron Taylor

Cameron Taylor

16 Meadow Street   Tempo, New York 02215   (914) 666-3654

This fine, spunky actress called me last year and expressed her incredible frustration with the "business." She was having trouble getting a response to her letters and was at her wit's end. I suggested she try a letter that wasn't merely "nice" but revealed her crusty, out-front qualities and I came up with this one.

Several agents had a good chuckle and said, "Get the Tootsie girl in here!" You see, she created an identifiable "handle" for herself. Plus, the fun the agents had with the letter made them very receptive to her.

A good letter should reveal your personality and be memorable. Almost everyone appreciates a sense of humor—just be careful not to go beyond the pale . . .

Terry
Slavin

242 Greenwood Avenue
Counterpoint, California 90069
(213) 799-2244

12 October 1983

Mr. James Friedrich
Kenny Artists, Inc.
2043 Highland Boulevard
Counterpoint, California 90036

Dear Mr. Friedrich:

You are invited to attend, as my guest, a performance of *La Bohème* in which I sing the leading role of Rudolfo. The production is directed by Stuart Braden at the Pacific Opera Theatre, 1201 Elm Street.

I will perform the role Wednesday, October 26th and Saturday, October 29th. The curtain is at 8:00 p.m.

I'm enclosing an addressed postcard, which will reserve a ticket for you and a guest on the evening of your choice. If you will also indicate your seating preference, I will do my best to make you comfortable.

I hope you enjoy the opera. I'm looking forward to speaking with you soon.

Thank you for your interest.

Sincerely,

Terry Slavin

Encl.: postcard, photo, and résumé

Dear Terry:

Please reserve two tickets for

Mr. James Friedrich for the evening of

___ Wednesday, October 26th
___ Saturday, October 29th

for the performance of <u>La Bohème</u>

The Pacific Opera Theatre

1201 Elm Street

Counterpoint

1. I phone and establish contact by introducing myself and my ensemble, and I inquire about the presenter's working procedures and needs. If the presenter shows an interest, I close the conversation by telling him I'll put some materials in the mail (not before I get spellings of names and addresses).

2. That day, I type a letter thanking that person for taking time for me on the telephone. Via this cover letter, I provide more information and further introduction. I enclose a brochure and any important graphic materials with this letter.

3. Five days later, I phone as a follow-up to see if the packet has landed on the right desk and to inquire if any more information is needed.

Note: I keep explicit records (see Activity Chart) through each and all of these contacts. I note names, addresses, dates of communications, phone numbers, materials sent, response received.

A glance at this sheet tells me who and how many people I've contacted in a month, what materials I've sent (this is my inventory indicator), and what the response has been. What percentage of contacts become jobs?

ACTIVITY CHART

This statistical chart clues me into what I'm doing right or wrong, how active or lazy I've been, etc. It presents the real picture and cuts down on fantasy.

Date	Name/Address	Materials (Letters, Résumés, Pictures, Brochures, and Demo Cassettes)	Response

I never get on the phone again with that contact person without my activity chart to clue me in. (I also make little notes that help me remember the personality of the contact person.)

Now, don't misunderstand me, this doesn't work *all* the time. If you have an easy, warm style on the telephone, it can be a more personal way to first make contact (provided that person is receptive to your call). Sometimes, that person is even on the lookout for your materials and will be more tuned-in when he or she peruses them.

If the phone is public enemy number one on your list, you might want your materials and talent to speak first and make the person more receptive to you. *But* don't ever think you can mail things and wait for admiring phone calls. You *must* follow up with a phone call and test the waters. That person is expecting you to call him. After all, you know when he's likely to be in the office, but it's anyone's guess as to your schedule. Don't be afraid. You are not bothering anyone with a follow-up call.

I'm going to let you in on a little something I discovered. I've calculated the optimum segment of time when I've gotten the most response to my calls—between ten-thirty and eleven in the morning! Between nine and ten o'clock people are not in or haven't had their coffee. Give them time to conquer their resistance to a lot of work. Getting on toward four is too close to end-of-day responsibilities and quitting time, so try to call between ten-thirty and eleven-thirty a.m., or between two-thirty and three-thirty p.m.

Though a lot of managers and presenters work from their homes, don't call anyone after five unless so requested. These people take their business hours seriously and you risk their resenting your intrusion.

Most often, a receptionist will ask who you are and what the call is in reference to. Do not resent these inquiries; the person is doing his or her job and is sometimes in a position to help or hurt you. You should be warm, natural, and responsive to anyone you happen to speak with.

One more thing. In all the years of calling people, finding them out of the office and having the receptionist offer to have my call returned, I've had it returned only a handful of times and when the person called and found out *I* had a request, the situation rapidly turned sour. Remember, you are the one who wants to establish contact, so don't shift the responsibility onto the other person. No matter how insistent the receptionist is, I only ask that he or she take my name and relay the message that I'll call again later.

BEFORE THE BEEP

Okay. Now you know how and when to contact them. How do they contact *you?* This brings us to a discussion of answering machines and answering services.

Back when I did the audition for *The King and I,* I had neither of the above and simply assumed the casting personnel would keep trying me. Please believe me, it wasn't narcissism, it was naïveté. I quickly found out that casting people have a list; if they can't reach you they go on to the next person. No one can afford to make it difficult for an employer to get in touch. So, it's up to you to purchase a machine or service.

A few years ago, when answering machines were not so commonplace, people argued in favor of a service. The theory was that a service provides a human voice, people don't leave messages on tape and presumably, a service could reach the artist (and vice versa) anytime, anywhere. However, there are humans who work for services who can't get messages straight and are indifferent to their urgency. Your machine will not sabotage you in those respects. And, to be candid about it, I opted for a machine because I didn't want to bother a service every ten minutes and be humiliated with the phrase, "Sorry, no calls." Now, in the privacy of my own home, I can listen to blank tape!

Today's answering machines come with a wide range of useful features. You must get one with a remote so you can call in from outside and retrieve your messages. Make sure you keep a record of how many dimes you anxiously deposit pursuing this activity—it can add up to over a hundred dollars a year and is tax-deductible as a business expense.

Talk to your friends, shop the stores, and consult your budget, but your machine or service is essential and indispensable. I like machines that flash a red light if there are calls; if possible, purchase one that is voice activated and does not record hang-ups. (These have driven me crazy through the years.)

So, let's say you opt for a machine. Once you hook it up, you must record an outgoing message and this, to people who've not met you before, reveals quite a bit about you. So, be yourself and be creative, but remember, you're not auditioning to be a comedian. You are a performing artist. Think it through and come up with something within the parameters of good taste. If you try to be funny, you'll spend a lot of time coming up with toppers for bored friends (you really *should* be practicing) and you risk offending someone who has a "strictly business" style. Also, time the message so there is not a lot of "dead air" before the beep. People tend to start talking in a pause or balk at the wait and you won't receive their communication. Write your message and rehearse it a few times to test out the timing before you record.

> Sample message: Hi, this is Brian Whitehead.* I'm unable to come to the phone right now, but I'd like to return your call. If you leave your name, number, and a brief message *after* the tone, I'll get back to you as soon as possible. Thank you very much.

I have two more things to add to this conversation. Try to avoid a stiff, affected style of speech and (this is a personal pet peeve) don't record a snatch of music before your voice-over comes on. It doesn't really serve you (certainly not the music). We know you're a musician, you know it, so what's the point? The wrong message can hurt you. I was helping to cast a movie at Universal and I called an actress. The casting director had seen her the night before and I happened, serendipitously, to know her. The outgoing message that greeted me first thing that morning had the strangest music and a psychotic speech pattern. I would have hung up if I hadn't known her. She was being funny for her friends; it could have cost her a film contract.

One more thing: If you have a tendency to talk on the phone for substantial periods of time, you should think about a "call-waiting" service. If your manager or a casting person continually gets a busy signal, he may get annoyed and skip over your name to get on with business.

YOUR BUSINESS CARD—PAPER PANACHE

If all is clear about the projection of your visual and audible image, let me touch briefly on one more "finishing" accessory—your business card. Yes, for a while I fought becoming *that* establishment, but it's definitely a way to distribute your name, address, and phone number with panache and practicality.

SPEAKING OF PRACTICALITIES

> ☑ Before visiting your stationer, collect other people's cards and decide what appeals to you—kind of type, stock, color of print. Again, ensure legibility and don't choose anything too crazy. Gray lettering on cream stock has a sharp look, still on the tasteful

---

*"You have reached 765-6821" is an option if you hesitate to announce your name.

end of things. Also, don't forget you can print on the diagonal or vertical or print the type flush to one side for a look with flair. A photo might say a lot for you, but it will cost a bit more. If you use the same color pattern and type for your stationery and your card, you develop a more "identifiable" you. And that's definitely what you're after.

☑ Don't choose a nonstandard size as many people store cards in holders—something too bulky may be roughed up or discarded.

☑ And while you're obsessed with just the right look for your card, purchase a stylish business card case from which to present it.

PROFESSIONAL APPEARANCE

Now that you look professional on paper and sound terrific on the telephone, let's make sure you don't disappoint in person. I don't want to play Pygmalion (or worse yet, sound like your mother) but I want to make sure nothing is missing from your total presentation. And that includes *you!* You are the backdrop for your talent. Wouldn't it be awful if your stationery made a better impression than you did?

The minute you enter a room to audition or meet someone for the first time, you put your credibility and sense of self-esteem on the line. A personal style implies that you know who you are and how you want to present yourself. And it earns you a certain respect. Here again we have the appearance/competency correlation, and an appropriate and professional personal presentation emphasizes your regard for quality. It often surprises me that so many musicians pamper and protect their instruments but forget to accord themselves the same treatment. Odd, when you think of it. Each one of you is a Stradivarius—just some of you don't know it yet!

It's a given that you'll be spending money on clothing and haircuts the rest of your life and it just doesn't make sense to adopt an ad hoc attitude toward the decisions. You can't go wrong though, if the words classic, elegant, and stylish can be applied to everything you do and wear. The idea is to strike a midpoint that doesn't go too far over to flair (it would be distracting) but takes a definite detour from drab. If you are well groomed, your dress or suit flatters your face and figure, and the colors you choose make you come alive, you'll make a favorable first impression and the people with the votes will sit up and listen. Plus, you'll know you

Diana List
5842 Chestnut Street
Grand Fugue, Michigan 49260
(616) 752-4691

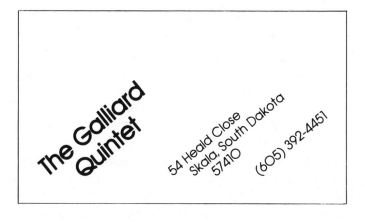

The Galliard Quintet

54 Heald Close
Skala, South Dakota
57410

(605) 392-4451

Kenneth Young

312 Old Post Road
Phonola, Texas 78340
(214) 865-3212

look good, there will be an added bounce to your step, and you'll be ready to get down to the serious business of displaying your talent.

So take a look through these questions and see if anything can be improved upon.

1. Have you found that special suit or dress that makes you look smart and exciting? Does the color enhance your skin tones and bring you to your best? How is the tailoring? Make sure nothing is too tight and that the lines lengthen and slim your figure. A princess line, non-blouson, unbelted dress will accomplish this for women. A coat and pants of the same material and color will do a lot to make a man appear taller and slimmer. Try to buy clothing that is as wrinkle-resistant as possible, but keep in mind that quality fabrics look better and last longer. For an excellent discussion on clothing guidelines for daytime auditions, I suggest you read *The Art of the Song Recital* by Shirlee Emmons and Stanley Sonntag. It's published by Schirmer Books.

2. Does your hair always look neat and becoming? Is the style appropriate for auditions or does it get in the way? Stray strands that stick in your lipstick or locks that have to be tossed back constantly are uncomfortable, distracting, and make you look unprofessional. Get professional opinions about styles that are right for you and your situation, and learn how to do them quickly and effortlessly. And while I'm directing this to the female audience, let me mention the subject of makeup. By all means wear it. But wear it well. I suggest that you ask your photographer to recommend a makeup artist who could analyze your features and skin tones and teach you, in a quiet setting, how to apply makeup correctly. Try to avoid department stores as you cannot concentrate and the person doing your face is often more interested in enhancing his commission checks than you. Another option would be to check some of the salons nearby—some of them have makeup artists on staff. If your only option is a department store, try to go first thing on a weekday morning when the store is not likely to be so crowded and noisy.

3. How about those fingernails? A musician's hands are often in the limelight.

4. Did you remember to polish your shoes? Did you have them reheeled recently?

5. Do you arrive at auditions in a mixed and unmatched coat, scarf, hat, and gloves ensemble and hope no one notices? This outerwear should add to your professional image, not unbundle it. A lot of people recommend carrying shoes to the audition and therefore avoiding puddles and broken heels, but everything else you wear to an audition should be worn going in. No hangers, garment bags, and desperate requests for secluded rooms. Remember, you are a performing artist, not a quick-change one.

6. Does the bag you carry your music/instrument in look as if the rest of your wardrobe could be taken along for the ride? An oversized, unstructured bag will not convey a professional look and you'll be digging endlessly to locate things. I would recommend a good leather portfolio or briefcase. It is more expensive, but a well-made piece will accompany you for years.

7. Does your jewelry complement and finish your look? An unfinished look communicates a sense of being harried and unprepared. You want to communicate composure and polish. Tie clips, cufflinks, watches, rings, earrings, necklaces, and scarves should be simple, quality items. Be careful of bracelets that make noise and distract. Again, I would suggest removing religious jewelry.

8. What about your business card and credit card cases, wallet, checkbook, appointment book, and eyeglass case? Don't forget that they are all part of your wardrobe and do so often see the light of day. They should reflect your regard for quality. How about that pen you use? Does it scream the name and phone number of your dry cleaner? I want you to sign your contracts with an elegant writing tool.

9. When you leave the room after an audition, does the scent of you linger longer than the thought? Every auditioner I spoke to mentioned that people pour on the perfume and aftershave and leave the jury cooped up in a room all day with Tea Rose, Old Moss, and Resentment with a capital R. Go easy on the bottle!

10. Women, don't forget to bring an extra pair of stockings (a run will run your mood straight into the ground). Also, tuck an emery board into your bag, and if you wear polish on your nails, bring it along for emergency touch-ups. Males and females should bring along a needle and thread to fix that errant button or unruly hem.

You, the performer, are a vital ingredient in the phenomenon of music and you have a lot to say. Often though, you'll have to say it first on paper, over the telephone, or at an initial meeting. Let everything that comes from you reflect your professional attitude and tilt the circumstances in your favor. If you can get people to look up, it won't be long before you can get them to listen.

CHAPTER 5

United We Stand: Union Affiliations

PERFORMERS' UNIONS, FOR THE MOST PART, negotiate contracts and establish performance pay scales, lobby for better legislation, limit rehearsal hours, protect artists from the unscrupulous, and often offer pension, health, and welfare benefits to their membership. The type of musician you are or the kind of job you're playing will determine which union you will be eligible to join.

The first movie soundtrack I sang fell under the jurisdiction of the Screen Actors Guild (SAG), of which I was not a member. I was hired by the contractor and was able to do the job thanks to the Taft-Hartley Law. This law states that a person can work for a period of time on a union job without having to join that union. Usually, one can work up to thirty calendar days on a first job, but on the second job, or any job secured after the thirty calendar days, or any job that lasts more than thirty days, one *has* to join the union or forfeit the right to work the job. Note that the Taft-Hartley Law applies to certain unions in certain states.

Because I had done a union job, I was then eligible to become a union member (and thrilled at the prospect). You've all heard the "Catch-22" complaints that sound like this: "You can't audition for the union job without having a union card, but you can't get the union card without having a contract for the job." While this *is* in a sense true in certain cases, there *are* pathways to becoming a member of even the most restrictive union. Let's straigten this all out.

There are nine performers' unions that make up the Associated Actors and Artistes of America (known as *the 4 A's*). Five of these nine concern us here—they are:

AGMA—American Guild of Musical Artists

AFTRA—American Federation of Television and Radio Artists

AGVA—American Guild of Variety Artists

SAG—Screen Actors Guild

AEA—Actors' Equity Association

Outside the *4 A's* is the very important instrumentalists' union, The American Federation of Musicians. I'll discuss that later, but first let me give you a thumbnail sketch of the *4 A's*.

AGMA was founded in 1936 as an organization of solo musical artists, but came to embrace all performers in the opera, ballet, oratorio, concert, and recital fields. So if you are singing with the New York City Opera or the chorus of the Chicago Symphony, touring with the Gregg Smith singers, or are an apprentice at Wolf Trap (just to mention a few)—you are working under the jurisdiction of AGMA.

To join, you must be offered a contract by an AGMA employer, or already be a member of another 4A union, in which case your initiation fee and dues will be less. The initiation fee is on a sliding scale, based on your income. There is a $100.00 floor and a $200.00 ceiling.

Dues are also assessed according to income. A Pension and Welfare Fund is offered through participating employers. The union also offers a group Major Medical, Dental, and Life Insurance plan, legal and professional advice and a Relief Fund.

AFTRA has jurisdiction over all performers (exclusive of instrumentalists) working in live and taped TV shows, taped commercials and industrials, radio shows, and phonograph records. Contracts are negotiated and based on type, length, and category of program.

To join, you must pay only the initiation fee and dues. The current initiation fee is $600.00. The base assessment of dues is $28.75, twice a year—in May and November. This amount escalates with a rise in professional income.

AGVA has jurisdiction over a variety of *live* performers, ranging from circus clowns to night club performers.

AGVA is an open union. To join, you simply must satisfy the union that you are a working performer, pay the $300.00 initiation fee and the first 6 months' dues. Dues are paid three times a year on an escalating basis. If you are a member of another 4A union, you can become an AGVA member at half the initiation fee.

AEA, also called Equity, has jurisdiction over performers and stage managers in legitimate theatre productions of musicals and dramas. There are now only two ways to become a member of Equity:

1. You must be hired to work in an Equity show and given an Equity contract. You present the contract to Equity, pay the $500.00 initiation fee and the first six months' dues of $26.00, and you receive an Equity card as soon as the paper work is processed. Dues are paid twice yearly, in November and May, and the base assessment is $52.00. When you begin working, you pay 2 percent of your contractual salary as dues, up to a maximum of $2,000.00.

2. You join an Equity Membership Candidate Program at one of a number of participating Equity theatres. You then earn credit with your work toward AEA membership. Fifty weeks of such work are required, though they need not be consecutive.

You cannot "buy" into Equity from another parent union, but if you fulfill the above requirements and are a member of another entertainment industry union, you can join Equity for a reduced fee.

For further information, contact the Membership Division.

SAG has jurisdiction over performers working in feature films, filmed TV shows, filmed commercials and industrial films. To join, you must have a principal contract in a filmed union production, or be hired as a stunt player. If you are cast in a TV commercial, you don't have to have lines, but must be a principal player as outlined in the SAG Commercial Contract in order to become eligible for union membership.

The initiation fee is $600.00 and dues are assessed on the preceding year's professional earnings. The base for dues is $37.50, payable in May and November.

If you are a currently paid-up member of one of the *4 A's* for a period of one year or longer and have worked as a *principal* in the jurisdiction of that union, you will be eligible for SAG membership at a reduced initiation fee.

The American Federation of Musicians is an international organization with over 500 Local affiliates in the United States and Canada. The constitution reads, "All performers on musical instruments of any kind and vocalists, or other individuals who render musical services of any kind for pay, are classed as professional musicians and are eligible for membership." To join, you apply for membership in the local in your own area of residence. Each local is autonomous and sets its own fees and dues. Being a member of a local affiliates you with the national organization which negotiates contracts and national tours and provides pension, health, and welfare benefits.

WHERE TO WRITE OR CALL

No doubt you have many questions about union affiliations and all that they offer, request, and require. Give a call to one of these national or regional offices and speak to the membership department:

AGMA

(National Office)
1841 Broadway
New York NY 10023
(212)265-3687

(Canada)
615 Yonge St.
Toronto Ont. M4Y 2T4
(416)967-4252

(Chicago)
307 N. Michigan Ave.
Chicago IL 60601
(312)372-8081

(Los Angeles)
Suite 205, 12650 Riverside Dr.
N. Hollywood CA 91607
(213)877-0683
(213)984-3950

(New England)
11 Beacon St.
Boston MA 02108
(617)742-0208

(New Orleans)
34 San Jose Ave.
Jefferson LA 70121
(504)835-4180

(Northwest)
#202, 2253 Gilman Dr. W.
Seattle WA 98119
(206)282-0804

(Philadelphia)
Lafayette Building, 8th Floor
5th and Chestnut St.
Philadelphia PA 19106
(215)925-8400

(San Francisco)
Suite 1500, 100 Bush St.
San Francisco CA 94104
(415)986-4060

(Texas)
3915 Fairlakes Dr.
Dallas TX 75228
(214)279-4720

(Washington, DC)
Suite 204, 2700 "Q" St.
Washington DC 20007
(202)337-8688

AFTRA

(National Office)
1350 Avenue of the Americas
New York NY 10019
(212)265-7700

(Arizona)
#301, 3030 N. Central
Phoenix AZ 85012
(602)279-9975

(California)
Apt. D, 822 Terrace Place
Madera CA 93637
(209)674-1039

1717 N. Highland Ave.
Hollywood CA 90028
(213)461-8111

#308, 3045 Rosecrans St.
San Diego CA 92110
(619)222-1161

c/o KOVR-TV
1216 Arden Way
Sacramento CA 95815
(916)927-1313

100 Bush St.
San Francisco CA 94104
(415)391-7510

(Colorado)
#639, 6825 E. Tennessee
Denver CO 80224
(303)388-4287

(Connecticut)
c/o Station WSTC
117 Prospect St.
Stamford CN 06901
(203)327-1400

(District of Columbia)
#608, 4201 Connecticut Ave., N.W.
Washington DC 20026
(202)363-9740

(Florida)
#102, 1450 N.E. 123rd St.
North Miami FL 33161
(305)891-0779

(Georgia)
#210, 3110 Maple Dr. N.E.
Atlanta GA 30305
(404)237-0831
(404)237-9961

(Hawaii)
Box 1350
Honolulu HI 96807
(808)533-2652

(Illinois)
307 N. Michigan Ave.
Chicago IL 60601
(312)372-8081

Station WEEK
2907 Springfield Rd.
E. Peoria IL 61611
(309)699-5052

(Indiana)
Yosha & Cline
7th Floor, 2220 N. Meridian St.
Indianapolis IN 46208
(317)925-9200

(Kentucky)
#250, 730 W. Main St.
Louisville KY 40202
(502)584-6594

(Louisiana)
808 St. Anne
New Orleans LA 70116
(504)524-9903

(Maryland)
#1145, 10 Light St.
Baltimore MD 21202
(301)752-6160

(Massachusetts)
#1000, 11 Beacon St.
Boston MA 02108
(617)742-0208
(617)742-2688

(Michigan)
#406, Heritage Plaza Office Building
24901 N. Western Hwy.
Southfield MI 48075
(313)354-1774

(Minnesota)
Suite A, 2500 Park Ave. S.
Minneapolis MN 55404
(612)871-2404

(Missouri)
#310, 406 W. 34th St.
Kansas City MO 64111
(816)753-4557

Paul Brown Bldg.
#1237, 818 Olive St.
St. Louis MO 63101
(314)231-8410

(New York)
c/o Station WROW-AM
341 Northern Blvd.
Albany NY 12204
(518)436-4841

WIVB-TV
2077 Elmwood Ave.
Buffalo NY 14207
(716)874-4410

#900, One Exchange St.
Rochester NY 14614
(716)232-1540

170 Ray Ave.
Schenectady NY 12304
(518)385-1267

(Ohio)
1814-16 Carew Tower
Cincinnati OH 45202
(513)579-8668

1367 E. 6th St.
#229, The Lincoln Bldg.
Cleveland OH 44114
(216)781-2255

1580 Berkshire Rd.
Columbus OH 43221
(614)481-8479

(Oregon)
915 N.E. Davis St.
Portland OR 97232
(503)238-6914

(Pennsylvania)
#811, 1405 Locust St.
Philadelphia PA 19102
(215)732-0507

The Penthouse, 625 Stanwix St.
Pittsburgh PA 15222
(412)281-6767

(Tennessee)
1108 17th Ave. S.
Acklen Station, Box 121087
Nashville TN 37212
(615)327-2947

(Texas)
#102, 3220 Lemmon Ave.
Dallas TX 75204
(214)522-2080
(214)522-2085

#214, 2620 Fountainview
Houston TX 77057
(713)982-1806

(Washington)
158 Thomas St.
Box 9688
Seattle WA 98109
(206)624-7340

(Wisconsin)
929 52nd St.
Kenosha WI 53140

AGVA: EAST & WEST COAST OFFICES

184 Fifth Ave.
New York NY 10010
(212)675-1003

4741 Laurel Canyon Blvd.
N. Hollywood Ca 91607
(213)508-9984

SAG

(National Office)
7750 Sunset Blvd.
Hollywood Ca 90046
(213)876-3030

(Arizona)
#919, 3030 N. Central
Phoenix AZ 85012
(602)279-9975

(California)
#308, 3045 Rosecrans
San Diego Ca 92110
(714)222-3996

26th Floor, 100 Bush St.
San Francisco CA 94104
(415)391-7510

(Colorado)
#639, 6825 E. Tennessee Ave.
Denver CO 80222
(303)388-4287

(Florida)
#317, 145 Madeira Ave.
Coral Gables FL 33134
(305)444-7677

(Georgia)
#210, 3110 Maple Dr. N.E.
Atlanta GA 30305
(404)237-9961

(Illinois)
307 N. Michigan Ave.
Chicago IL 60601
(312)372-8081

(Maryland—serves D.C.)
210, 35 Wisconsin Circle
Chevy Chase MD 20015
(301)657-2560

(Massachusetts)
#1000, 11 Beacon St.
Boston MA 02108
(617)742-2688

(Michigan)
28690 Southfield Rd.
Lathrup Village MI 48076
(313)559-9540

(Minnesota)
Suite A*, 2500 Park Ave.
Minneapolis MN 55402
(612)871-2404

(Missouri)
#310*, 406 W. 34th St.
Kansas City MO 64111
(816)753-4557

#617*, 818 Olive St.
St. Louis MO 64111
(314)231-8410

(New York)
18th Floor, 1700 Broadway
New York NY 10019
(212)957-5370

(Ohio)
1367 E. 6th St.*
Cleveland OH 44114
(216)781-2255

(Pennsylvania)
#811, 1405 Locust St.*
Philadelphia PA 19102
(215)545-3150

(Tennessee)
1108 17th Ave. S.
Nashville TN 37212
(615)327-2944

(Texas)
#102, 3220 Lemmon Ave
Dallas TX 75204
(214)522-2080

#215, 2620 Fountainview
Houston TX 77057
(713)972-1806

(Washington)
158 Thomas St.*
Seattle WA 98109
(206)624-7340

AEA

(National Office)
165 W. 46th St.
New York NY 10036
(212)869-8530

(Western)
#616, 6430 Sunset Blvd.
Hollywood CA 90028
(213)462-2334

Suite 1500, 100 Bush St.
San Francisco CA 94104
(415)986-4060

(Midwest)
#1401, 360 N. Michigan Ave.
Chicago IL 60601
(312)641-0393

AF OF M

In order to obtain further information and the address and phone number of the local in your area, call the National/International Office:

(212)869-1330
or toll free (800)223-6624
1500 Broadway
New York NY 10036

*AFTRA offices which handle SAG for their area.

ON YOUR WAY

CHAPTER 6

Achieving Your Graphic Image

I WAS DISCUSSING the contents of this book with someone in the music business, and as I began to describe this chapter, he asked me with some impatience, "What do musicians have to know about graphics? What matters is how they sound."

Ah, yes—but the sound of your music may never fill the air if the graphic materials preceding you represent you poorly. Good graphic design can generate interest in you and your artistry. A well-designed brochure or recital flyer or press kit will organize the information, get your message across and imprint a dynamic impression of you in the reader's mind.

Therefore, the intention of this chapter is to acquaint you with the terms, procedures, and options you'll encounter with your graphic designer, typesetter, and printer. These craftsmen, along with your personal taste and knowledge of *your* market, will give birth to a piece that speaks well for you. Afterward we'll talk about your relationship with the United States Postal Service.

THE GRAPHIC DESIGNER

A graphic designer is a person with imaginative talent and technique. After listening to your needs and desires, he or she will design the piece, order the type and prepare the mechanical, and explicitly specify the job to the printer. You will be billed for the design concepts, the typesetting, photostats, mechanical preparation, follow-through and printing costs.

You find a graphic designer in about the same way you found a photographer: by talking to people. Once you collect a few names of designers in your price category, make appointments and review their portfolios. If your budget barely covers the printing and mailing expenses, you might want to talk to some talented students in local art schools or universities. They would probably be enthusiastic about your project because they need to build a portfolio to launch *their* careers. If you decide to go this route, give a call to the head of the art department—he or she will no doubt be happy to recommend someone.

Once you settle on a graphic designer, it will be up to *you* to inform him of your taste and style, the market you need to reach, the information that must be conveyed, *your deadlines,* and (can't escape this one) your budget limitations. You can prepare for your first meeting by typing out an approximate indication of all copy to be included, deciding which photos you want to feature, and collecting brochures/flyers/mailers that appeal to you. Go into any major concert hall or music store and pick up ones you like and dislike. You'll soon be able to isolate styles of print, color combinations, and paper stocks that match your taste. The more you define yourself to and communicate with the designer, the closer he will come to answering your needs.

It will help you to determine your tastes if you understand the lay of the land concerning color, paper stock, and type styles.

BLACK IS A COLOR?

When used appropriately, color can create a more eye-catching piece and give you more options in design.

There are two basic processes involved in color reproduction: matched color and four-color process. Four-color process gives photographs a true-to-life color. It also gives you a bigger-than-life bill, so I'll only discuss matched color.

Your matched-color piece can contain one to four colors, but keep in mind that there's an additional cost for each additional color. A clarinetist recently described her ensemble's brochure to me as a black-and-white, no-color piece. This is a common misconception—black ink is considered a color like any other. So hers was a one-color job. You could gain a bit of flexibility with no extra cost, though, by printing one color of ink on a colored stock.

You should also know about the possibility of using a *Benday screen.* This allows you to introduce tonalities and tints into your piece by printing inks at a percentage of their full color. Thus, a Benday screen of black produces gray, of red produces pink.

You and your designer will decide on the color schemes and precisely communicate this information to the printer by referring to the Pantone Matching System (PMS). This is a standardized system of over 500 colors. These swatch books show colors printed on both coated and uncoated paper, so remember that the color you choose will be affected by the finish of the stock you print it on. Color stocks may slightly darken an ink color.

. . . THE PAPER IT'S PRINTED ON

The weight, opacity, and finish of a stock are important considerations, so we'll take a minute to define them.

Weight: Brochures are usually printed on sixty-, seventy-, or eighty-pound text-weight stock, a type of book paper.

You will want your brochure to feel substantial but not bulky. A piece that folds can have a lighter weight because the folding process causes the paper to "bulk up," thus giving it a heavier feel. If you are planning a flyer to be mailed third class, you will have to watch the weight as it must be under 3.911 ounces and less than one fourth of an inch thick.

Opacity: The ability of the paper to take ink without "see through" on the reverse side.

Finish: Paper comes with either a coated or uncoated surface.

Uncoated (or matte) paper is mostly used for jobs that have no photographs.

Coated paper (sometimes called enamel) has a special coating that fills in any unevenness and gives the paper a smooth, slick surface. Because of this, the ink rests on the paper's surface, yielding a sharper, more brilliant image. Coated paper may have a dull or glossy finish.

Now, photographs and color reproduce more brilliantly on a coated paper, but its reflectivity makes reading text slightly more difficult. A gloss paper may give a slick, "cool" look to a piece or it may read "tacky."

Decide which is more important, the photo or the message (often the photo *is* the message) and give a lot of thought to the tone of the piece.

Along these lines, I had a pianist friend who was using a full length photo of herself in a black velvet dress for a debut recital mailer. The folds of the dress did not print sharply on an uncoated paper, so she chose a coated finish. It worked extremely well.

IMPORTANT! If you use a pen to write on a glossy paper, the ink will smudge. Therefore, if your flyer requires a return response, look to an uncoated stock.

Also, a coated stock may crack when folded against the grain, so make sure the printer cuts his paper with the grain in the proper direction. Not too long ago, I unfolded a recital flyer printed against the grain and there was a horizontal white crack decapitating the artist!

TRUE TO TYPE

Chances are, you've been reading printed material since childhood without paying attention to the style of the letters on the page. Now it's time to pay attention. There are hundreds of styles of type, and each has a distinct personality. A typeface can be old-fashioned or futuristic, understated or gaudy, strong or soft, classic or avant-garde. The typeface you choose will affect the total look of the piece and convey a subliminal message that reflects back on you. Keep in mind that some decorative faces are difficult to read when used to set a block of text.

Many typefaces come with variations: roman or *italic*, lightface, **boldface, *bold italic***. A typeface with all of its variations is called a type *family*, and use of one family can preserve a unity of design while allowing flexibility.

Type families can be mixed for more visual interest. For examples of this, pick up the nearest magazine and look at the advertisements. In many of them you will see that the headline grabbing your attention is set in one face, while the smaller "sell copy" hyping the product is in another. (You'll notice also that the face used in an ad for steel-belted radials is different from one used to sell perfume.) Like colors, typefaces can complement or clash with one another, so let good taste and the advice of your designer be your guide.

Nearly all type fits into one of two categories—*serif* or *sans serif*. Serifs are the fine lined cross-strokes at the top and bottom of letters. Serif styles are easy and pleasant to read in large masses, which is why most newspapers, books, and magazines are set in this category of type.

Sans serif has no cross-strokes and gives a more modern look. If there is not a large amount of copy, it does not present a problem. A large block of some sans serif types can look cold, sterile, and forbidding to read, however.

Samples of popular typefaces

Times Roman (serif) For the love of music
Helvetica (sans serif) For the love of music
Souvenir (serif) For the love of music

Remember two more things: Copy that is set in all capital letters is difficult to read. This is because the top silhouette of capital letters is basically a rectangle with few variations to make word recognition easy. Avoid much use of ALL CAPS *and use italics sparingly.*

A publicist once specified a publicity piece for my ensemble in italics, as she felt it was "warmer and more personal." Once I got to the typesetter, though, I began waffling about the choice and complained that I couldn't *read* italics. Chewing my fingernails, I plunged ahead and told the typesetter to give me the copy in Century Roman. Later I found out that italics are usually too light for effective readability in large quantities and should be reserved only for accent. Save your manicure!

A WAY WITH WORDS

Keeping all this in mind, collect samples of pieces you like and get ready for the first meeting with your designer. First, however, check the copy you've written and, if the piece is to advertise an event, be sure it includes the following information:

- Your name

- Name of ensemble or group

- Date of event—day of the week and calendar date; Saturday, May 7, 1983

- Time of event—with a.m. or p.m.

- Place and address of event

- Ticket information, prices, discounts if any

- Phone number for reservations and information

- Subscription coupon (if applicable)

- Descriptive or selling copy, quotes, bios, etc.

- Indication of manager or presenter (if applicable)

- Program to be performed

- Special credits (photo, funding, design)

- Indicia (described later on)

- Return address

If you're not a born writer, you may need some help finding just the right words for the selling copy and bios. Ask your fellow musicians who it was that wrote the snappy copy in their brochures, or call upon your own network of family and friends. For do-it-yourselfers, there is no better guide to the basics of writing than *The Elements of Style* by William Strunk and E.B. White.

Now, with your more educated eye for graphics, you're ready for your first meeting with your chosen graphic designer. Your designer will look at the amount of copy and number of photographs and begin to make decisions about the size and folds of the piece. Folding allows for the isolation and organization of information in different sections. The sketches below depict some popular folds for brochures:

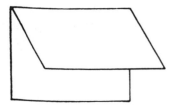

Four-page folder (fold along short dimension)

Four-page folder (fold along long dimension)

Six-page folder (two parallel folds)

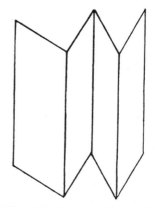

Eight-page folder with three parallel accordion folds

At the second meeting, the designer will present you with several to-scale, rough drafts of your possible piece. *Now* is the time to speak up and suggest changes if there is anything you don't like. Make sure the piece sells *you* and not the designer's talent; people seeing it should say, "I'd like to hear this musician," not "My, what a clever brochure."

Once you opt for IT, the designer will begin the series of steps that will end in the completed piece. A *mechanical*—the paste-up of all type, line art and indications of photo positions—must be prepared for the printer. These steps are interesting and you should understand the pre-production service your designer is performing for you.

First, the designer must order the type from the typesetter. He's going to have to specify the type face to be used, the size (measured in points), the length of lines (measured in picas) and the spacing between lines (called leading, pronounced "ledding" and measured in points). There are twelve points to a pica and six picas to an inch.

6   7   8   9   10   11   12

14   18   24   30   36

For example, your name on your flyer might be 36 points (this means that if your name is Mary, the space from the top of the capital M to the tip of the descender of the y will measure half an inch) while a photo credit might be 10 (just over one-eighth of an inch). The designer would indicate how each section would be set and would use a shorthand that looks like this: TR 10/12-16½.

This means the copy should be set in Times Roman, 10 point, with 2-point leading, 16½ picas wide. The typesetter would send back this:

> Speak the speech, I pray you, as I pronounced it to you, trippingly on the tongue; but if you mouth it, as many of your players do, I had as lief the town-crier spoke my lines. Nor do not saw the air too much with your hand, thus; but use all gently: for in the very torrent, tempest, and as I may say the whirlwind of passion, you must acquire and beget a temperance, that may give it smoothness. Oh, it offends me to the soul to hear a robustious periwig-pated fellow tear a passion to tatters, to very rags, to split the ears of the groundlings, who for the most part are capable of nothing but inexplicable dumb-shows and noise. I would have such a fellow whipped for o'erdoing Termagant; it out-herods Herod.
>
> *Hamlet:* act 3, scene 2

This book has been set in 10/13 Palatino.

In all probability, the type would be set on a photo-typesetting system. This is a computer with a keyboard and photo-unit. (Here we're speaking of typewriter, not piano, keyboards.) The photo-unit includes a master character image, a light source and a photo- or light-sensitive material. There are special keys on the keyboard that allow the typesetter to program fonts, leading, letterspacing, etc. A perforated tape, magnetic tape, or magnetic disc is produced.

After the copy has been keyboarded, the tape or disc is fed into the photo-unit. This triggers a selection of characters from a master character set and a burst of light is flashed through the character. This beam of light is then deflected by mirrors and prisms and projected onto photosensitive paper or film. The point size of the type can be enlarged or reduced by lenses built into the system.

Photograph courtesy of Compugraphic Corporation

After the type has been set, the typesetter will send your designer a reader's (or galley) proof. He will check it and send it on to you. Get out your glasses and your dictionary and read it carefully. Then pass it on to friends to proof it. A frequently overlooked error is an incorrect word break at the end of a line. If the type is set *justified* (flush left and right) a word will be broken from time to time. Look these up!

If the type is unjustified—for example, *ragged right*, which means only the left side is flush—no words should need to be broken. Look also for lines that areverytight or t o o s p a c e d o u t. Discuss all mistakes with your designer. He will mark them in the margin with the standard proofreading marks (see next page). Any mistakes made by the typesetter should be marked PE (printer's error). These are corrected free of charge. Any mistakes or changes you just now catch should be marked AA (author's alteration). You *will* be charged for these changes. This is *not* the time to rewrite!

Your designer will send the proofs back to the typesetter. All the alterations will be made and reproduction proofs returned to the designer. These will be used to create the *mechanical* of your piece.

Proofreader's Marks

MARK	EXPLANATION	(In margin.) EXAMPLE	(In text.)
ℓ	Take out character indicated.	ℓ	Your manuscrippt.
stet or ...	Let it stay.	stet	Your manuscript.
#	Put in space.	#	Yourmanuscript.
⁀	Close up completely.		Writer's Di gest School.
tr	Transpose; change places.	tr	Yuor manuscript.
caps or ≡	Use capital letters.	caps	writer's digest school. writer's digest school.
lc	Use lower-case letters.	lc	Your Manuscript.
bf or ~~~	Use bold-face type.	bf	Writer's Digest School. Writer's Digest School
ital or ___	Use italic type.	ital	Writer's Digest.
'	Put in apostrophe.	'	Writers Digest School.
⊙	Put in period.	⊙	Your manuscript
,/	Put in comma.	,/	Your manuscript
:/	Put in colon.	:/	Your manuscript
;/	Put in semicolon.	;/	Writer's Digest School
" "	Put in quotation marks.	" "	He said, Yes.
(?)	Question to author.	(?) No hyphen OK	Free lance writer.
=/	Put in hyphen.	=/	Free lance writer.
!	Put in exclamation.	!	This is great
?	Put in question mark.	?	Are you starting
(/)	Put in parenthesis.	(/)	Your first rough draft.
¶	Start paragraph.	¶	a writer. Learn to sell
‖	Even out lines	‖	Writer's Digest and Writer's Digest School.
⊏	Move the line left		Your manuscript.
⊐	Move the line right		Your manuscript.
No ¶	No paragraph; run together	No ¶	a writer. There are more needed
out, sc	Something missing, see copy.	out, sc	Writer's School.
spell out	Spell it out.	spell out	Your ms.

ON TO THE MECHANICAL! OFF TO THE PRINTER!

The designer now creates a mechanical—a piece of illustration board which contains the copy, line art, and design elements pasted into position. The photographs are not pasted onto the mechanical, as they require special treatment by the printer. They will be mounted on separate boards, but their position and size are indicated on the mechanical with "holding lines" by the designer.

Creating a mechanical is a technically exacting job and I won't go into detail. However, once it is finished, your designer will cover it with tracing paper attached with masking tape. The tracing paper protects the mechanical and the designer can indicate ink colors, tint percentages, etc. on it. If there are two sides to a piece, there are two mechanicals. DO NOT WRITE ON MECHANICALS unless you've got a special, non-reproducing blue pencil. BE SURE YOUR HANDS ARE CLEAN before handling a mechanical. Do not eat your lunch on it, or swat flies with it, etc. Once the mechanicals are checked and rechecked by you and the designer, they are brought to the printer.

ON TO THE PRESS!

At last the printer has the mechanical and photos in his possession and may begin the final phase of creating your graphic piece. First, he must deal with the photographs. You see, the printing process is able to reproduce only solid tones from a single color ink. Type or line drawings are no problem, but what about photographs? These have many graduations of tones (for example, grays and middle tones) which cannot be reproduced except by a process known as *screening*. With this, the printer photographs the photograph through a *halftone* screen which converts the photo into a series of minute dots. The limited resolving power of the human eye is fooled by the optical illusion created and sees only a photograph. Examine closely any photograph in any newspaper and you'll see it's really a series of dots.

Note: Once a photo has been screened, it should not be rescreened. Therefore, you can't use a photo from a book or magazine. The photograph must be original art.

Invariably, the printer will reproduce your piece through a process known as *photo-offset* (also known as offset lithography or simply, offset). First, the printer takes a photograph of the mechanicals and screens all the photos. Then the negatives of the copy and photos are positioned onto a sheet of orange opaque paper (called goldenrod) and a *flat* is made. This flat is used to make a metal printing plate.

The offset process is based on the principle that grease and water don't mix. The image and the nonprinting area are on the same plane but their separation is maintained by a chemical treatment. The printed image areas must be grease (ink) receptive and water repellent; the nonprinting area must be water receptive and grease repellent. The plate is wrapped around the press and the inked image is transferred to a thin rubber blanket and then "offset" onto the paper which is feeding through.

Be aware of the fact that the printer can stop the press and erase from the plate, which can be an advantage to you. Let's say you decide to do a large mailing at the bulk rate, but realize that certain mailings must go out first class in order to arrive at the exact moment. You can instruct the printer to run off a certain number of mailers with the bulk rate indicia, stop the press, delete the indicia and run off the rest which you will meter or stamp. This way you can ensure your audience and save your budget at the same time.

Before your job is run off, however, the printer will send your designer a *blueprint* or blueline. This is a blue photographic print of your piece made from the flat. From this you can see that the photos are correctly placed. Once you and your designer give the go-ahead, the printer makes the plate and *the presses roll!*

So now you know a bit about the process and the people who make it happen. With this information under your belt, let's touch a bit on some editorial and design considerations that are seemingly subtle but make for a more effective piece.

FINE TUNING

First of all, you must assume that the reader has little time and less concentration. Therefore, the elements of your design must "leap up" to him and communicate quickly and easily. We're after a piece that brims with vitality and piques interest.

1. Clearly organize and pace the piece. If there is more than one side, think of the front as a cover or headline. Draw the reader in and then continue the introduction on the next page. The initial impact should be as strong and unified as possible. The typeface, photo, color, and spacing should feel like one integrated image.

    About the copy—don't bombard the reader with too much information. Be selective! Your mother may cherish every word written about you; a stranger will not. Here again, the philosophy mapped out in Chapter 2 prevails—less is more. *The object is to in-*

trigue, not satiate. Note: If you are listing a European tour, don't follow it with the description of a college engagement. *Don't dilute impressive credits!* Also avoid printing a substantial amount of copy in reverse type—white type on a color—it is difficult to read and will discourage anyone from doing so. However, in small doses it can be very dramatic.

2. Your picture is probably the most important part of the communication and it must project forward to the reader. Don't try to be part of an abstract, distant image. You are a personality selling a specific artistic point of view and only a natural human being can express that. Moreover, a human picture stirs the imagination of the person looking at it.

Choose a photo image of yourself which is strong and immediate. Your designer may suggest cropping, silhouetting, or bleeding to achieve this.

Cropping—the elimination of the unwanted part of the photograph by actually cutting it away.

Silhouetting—the mechanical whiting-out of the background. This makes the image appear to be jumping out from the page.

Bleeding—the placing of the photo so that it runs off one or more edges of the paper.

Photos facing into or toward copy lead the reader to the printed material. The title page picture can be straight out or facing right to induce people to turn the page. If you have a bad side, it doesn't matter. The printer can turn the negative and get your good side looking in at the copy. Also, research shows that one large photo on a cover is more effective than several smaller ones.

3. Amateur designers are often caught out by their ineffective use of white space. *White space* is an open, or blank, area on a graphic piece and is called *white* no matter what color paper you plan to use. White space can frame the copy and photos and make your piece look inviting and accessible. Amateurs often crowd every square pica of the paper with copy and art and produce a cluttered mess that no one will read. However, blank areas isolated or trapped in the middle of a layout will make the piece look disjointed and destroy what designers call "optical direction." A good designer knows how to balance white space with type, photographs, and other art to create an integrated graphic design.

4. The darker your paper stock, the less contrast and vitality your piece will have. White paper is crisp and dynamic; off-white or cream will have a traditional or classic connotation. The color of paper should not take over the piece.

5. If you decide to use more than one color of ink, make sure that one color is dominant. Don't choose two muted colors. Color is a totally subjective matter, but it definitely communicates a mood and tone, so give it a lot of thought.

IMPORTANT: Your name (or logo) must be as legible as possible. People remember it better and media personnel picking it up will have less cause to misspell it.

Your reviews, for my taste, can be set in italics. This change of typeface signals the reader that someone else is speaking about you—you, yourself, are not editorializing. A few quotes from good newspapers say more than a whole page of the same. Again, be selective.

JUST THREE MORE THINGS. I know I told you to inform your designer of your taste, but try not to be too rigid about it. Your photos and qualities may be better utilized when scrambled another way. Ask your designer to explain why he's doing something one way or the other. Also, make sure you get your mechanicals back and that you own full rights to the design and its various elements. A good logo will be of great use to you and you can reuse parts of the mechanical for future jobs.

Finally, keep explicit records of every printing job you do. Notate the designer, printer, specifications, number of copies, mailing method, and fees and costs. I keep a "Job Book," which is simply a three-hole binder with plastic sheet protectors. On one side I enclose the finished piece, and I fill in a form with all the specifications on the adjacent side.

I keep these records for the simplest photocopied announcements and programs as well as the most sophisticated design job. It's an important reference and it's a nice history of your progress as an artist.

Job: *Recital Flyer*
Date: *November 1983*

Designer: *Kevin Walz Design*
141 Fifth Avenue
New York, NY 10011
(212) 876-5432

Fee: _____

Typographer: *Not Just Type*
314 W. 52 Street
NYC 10019
(212) 664-1915

Fee: _____

Printer: *Scott Franz*
Varied Printing
6 Gwynns Mill Court
Owings Mills, MD 21117
(301) 363-2330

Mailing House: *Same*
_____
_____
_____

#	Description	Price
2,500	Flyers, 2 side print black and Pantone purple. 2 half-tones. Stymie Bold headings, Times Roman copy.	

Do I have mechanical? *yes*
Where? *3rd shelf of hall closet*

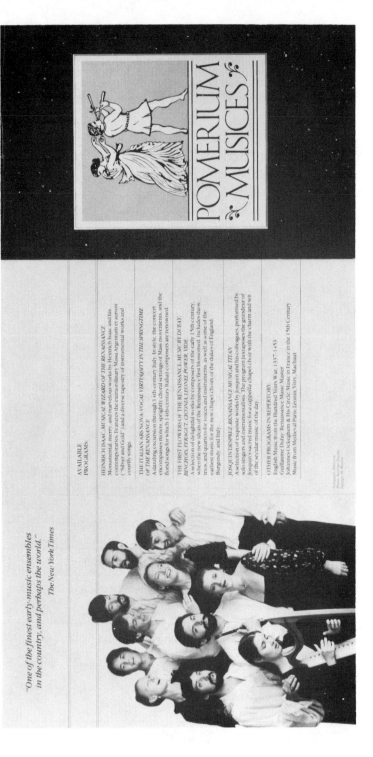

"One of the finest early-music ensembles in the country, and perhaps the world."
The New York Times

POMERIUM MUSICES

AVAILABLE PROGRAMS:

HEINRICH ISAAC: *MUSICAL WIZARD OF THE RENAISSANCE*
Monumental, merry, and marvelous works by Heinrich Isaac and his contemporaries. Features the extraordinary Missa Argentum et aurum ("Silver and Gold") and a diverse tapestry of instrumental works and courtly songs.

THE ITALIAN ARS NOVA: *VOCAL VIRTUOSITY IN THE SPRINGTIME OF THE RENAISSANCE*
A dazzling excursion through 14th-century Italy. In style, the concert encompasses motets, sprightly choral settings of Mass movements, and the florid songs for which 14th-century Italian composers are renowned.

THE FIRST FLOWERS OF THE RENAISSANCE: *MUSIC BY DUFAY, BINCHOIS, FRAGUT, GRENON, LIEBERT, POWER, VIDE*
A selection of delightful works by composers of the early 15th century, when the new ideals of the Renaissance first blossomed. Includes daring trios and quartets for voices and instruments, as well as some of the earliest music for the new chapel choirs of the dukes of England, Burgundy and Italy.

JOSQUIN DESPREZ: *RENAISSANCE MUSICAL TITAN*
A selection of exquisite works by Josquin and his colleagues, performed by solo singers and instrumentalists. The program juxtaposes the grandeur of Josquin's sacred music for a cappella chapel choir with the charm and wit of the secular music of the day.

OTHER PROGRAMS IN REPERTORY
English Music from the Hundred Years War: 1337-1453
Guillaume Dufay: Renaissance Music Master
Johannes Ockeghem & His Circle: Music in France in the 15th Century
Music from Medieval Paris: Léonin, Vitry, Machaut

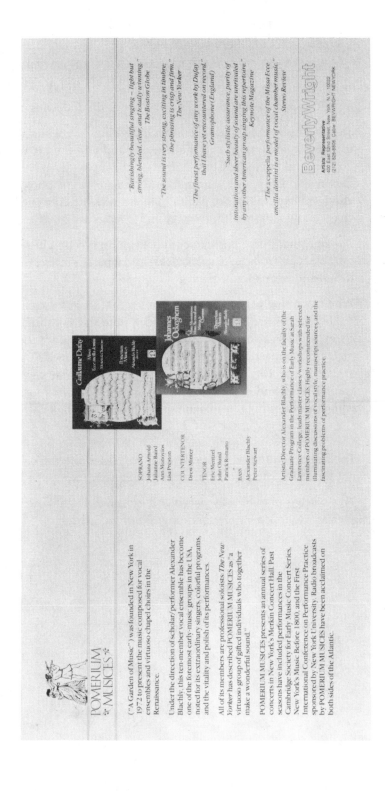

POMERIUM MUSICES

("A Garden of Music") was founded in New York in 1972 to present the music composed for vocal ensembles and virtuoso chapel choirs in the Renaissance.

Under the direction of scholar/performer Alexander Blachly, this ten-member vocal ensemble has become one of the foremost early-music groups in the USA, noted for its extraordinary singers, colorful programs, and the vitality and polish of its performances.

All of its members are professional soloists: *The New Yorker* has described POMERIUM MUSICES as "a virtuoso group of gifted individuals who together make a wonderful sound."

POMERIUM MUSICES presents an annual series of concerts in New York's Merkin Concert Hall. Past seasons have included performances in the Cambridge Society for Early Music Concert Series, New York's Music Before 1800, and the First International Conference on Performance Practice sponsored by New York University. Radio broadcasts by POMERIUM MUSICES have been acclaimed on both sides of the Atlantic.

SOPRANO
Johana Arnold
Julianne Baird
Ann Monoyios
Lisa Preston

COUNTERTENOR
Drew Minter

TENOR
Eric Mentzel
John Olund
Patrick Romano

BASS
Alexander Blachly
Peter Stewart

Artistic Director Alexander Blachly, who is on the faculty of the Graduate Program in the Performance of Early Music at Sarah Lawrence College, leads master classes/workshops with selected members of POMERIUM MUSICES. Highly recommended for illuminating discussions of vocal style, manuscript sources, and the fascinating problems of performance practice.

"Ravishingly beautiful singing – light but strong, blended, clear, and totally winning."
The Boston Globe

"The sound is very strong, exciting in timbre, the phrasing is crisp and firm."
The New Yorker

"The finest performance of any work by Dufay that I have yet encountered on record."
Gramophone (England)

"Such stylistic assurance, purity of intonation and sheer beauty of sound are unrivaled by any other American group singing this repertoire."
Keynote Magazine

"The a cappella performance of the Missa Ecce ancilla domini is a model of vocal chamber music."
Stereo Review

BeverlyWright
Artists' Representative
400 East 52nd Street, New York, N.Y. 10022
(212) 888-8806 Cable: BEVWRIGHT NEWYORK

ANALYSIS OF POMERIUM MUSICES BROCHURE

This brochure is an example of fine design for the following reasons:

The cover is simple, in a way rather intriguing. There's an air of antiquity to the illustration and the lettering and you want to open it up. You do, and the picture to the right is a triumph—ten people who reflect relationship, unity, humor, and humanity. The photo is silhouetted and it jumps off the page and teems with life. The one *New York Times* quote is large, impressive, and it *makes the point!*

The right-hand-side copy gives you some background in a large comfortable type. You can read it quickly and it piques interest. You want to see and hear them perform.

When you open the piece up completely (this is a six-page folder made with two regular, parallel folds), your eye goes to the record covers. This is a wonderful touch. I doubt that another photo could match the impact of the first and we aren't really ready for another one anyway. The record covers provide a different sort of graphic relief and impressively build another layer of information—this ensemble has been recorded on a fine label!

The last page to the right has five reviews listed the way I like them: not too many, not too long, and from equally impressive sources.

This piece is marvelously paced and executed. Highest accolades to designer M. Rollnik and photographer Norman Snyder.

Chesis/Cutler

The CHESIS/CUTLER flute and harp duo brings a lively refreshing new sound to the chamber music stage. In a repertoire which spans the centuries from the Renaissance to the present, this versatile duo challenges and entertains audiences with exciting interpretations of standard repertoire, commissioned new works, transcriptions, and even cabaret pieces.

Linda Chesis, flute, and Sara Cutler, harp, met at Tanglewood as teenagers, and their dynamic partnership has blossomed over a decade. Between them, these two Yale graduates have amassed a total of over thirty awards, scholarships, and competition victories. Their highly acclaimed New York recital debut in early 1982 established them as leading concert artists.

Linda Chesis was selected by Musical America Magazine as a "Young Artist of 1982." She studied with Jean-Pierre Rampal at the Paris Conservatory, where she took First Prize in flute. The only American prizewinner at the Paris International Flute Competition, she also won the first prize at the National Flute Association Competition in the U.S. Miss Chesis gave the world premiere of Bruce Saylor's *Turns and Mordents*, and has also performed it with the Houston Symphony.

She made her New York debut to a sold-out Carnegie Recital Hall in 1980, has been heard in recital on the Metropolitan Museum's Introduction Series, and as orchestral soloist in Carnegie Hall. Miss Chesis is an Affiliate Artist, Rotary scholar, and on the faculty of SUNY at Purchase, New York.

Sara Cutler's career has taken her through ten countries. She was soloist in the European premiere of Gian-Carlo Menotti's *Cantilena and Scherzo for Harp and Strings* at the Spoleto Festival of Two World's in Italy — a performance that was broadcast by Italian radio and filmed by the BBC.

She gave the British premiere performance of Malcolm Williamson's harp concerto at the Edinburgh Festival in Scotland. Her "unusually clear and precise" (American Record Guide) performance of Judith Zaimont's *Songs for Soprano and Harp* has been released by Leonarda Records. In the U.S., Miss Cutler has been concerto soloist at Town Hall in New York and at the Kennedy Center in Washington, D.C. A former pupil of Lucile Lawrence, Miss Cutler is on the faculty of Teacher's College, Columbia University.

Misses Chesis and Cutler are consistently praised not only for their intuitive sense of ensemble, but also for the articulate and engaging commentaries which are always part of their programs. Their numerous concerto engagements include appearances with Solisti New York, the Scottish Baroque Ensemble, and the Handel Society of Washington, D.C. The Chesis/Cutler Duo has appeared on major radio broadcasts in the U.S. and Europe, and is in great demand for master classes and workshops.

"Flutist Linda Chesis is a marvelous artist . . . outstanding in every way." THE NEW YORK TIMES

"An expert harpist . . . Sara Cutler portrayed a warm musical personality." THE NEW YORK TIMES

Chesis/Cutler

"Spirited and musically sophisticated." THE NEW YORK TIMES

CHESIS/CUTLER ANALYSIS

The "cover" of this brochure is a perfect example of a strong, unified image. The textures of the two women's dresses echo those of the harp, and the pattern of the flute keys is suggested again in the flutist's dress. It's really rich. Then, the *New York Times* quote is promising and you definitely want to turn the page.

And when you do! You see this heretofore glamorous concert duo in . . . jeans! They are humorous, *human* people and you really want to know them better. The pictures piqued my interest and prepared me for the read.

I won't deny there's a lot of copy here, but it's written in a fresh, warm style and the credentials are all so solid, I didn't feel I was reading filler or fluff.

The repetition of the name at the bottom of the page in outline is a nice change of tempo and the two reviews are cogent and to the point.

The design was by Donald Van Hook and the photos were taken by Christian Steiner. Bravo!

The Walter W. Naumburg Foundation
in co-operation with the Atlantic Richfield Foundation

presents

Paul Neubauer

Special Award 1982 Viola Competition

Wednesday, November 9, 1983, at 8:00 p.m.
Alice Tully Hall, Lincoln Center

Paul Neubauer,

Special award winner of the Walter W. Naumburg Foundation Viola Competition was born in Los Angeles in 1962. He has also been the recipient of the first prize in the Mae M. Whitaker International Competition for Strings, D'Angelo International Competition, and the Lionel Tertis International Viola Competition.

Mr. Neubauer has been heard with The Los Angeles Philharmonic, the San Francisco Symphony, and the English Chamber Orchestra, and has performed in recital in London's Wigmore Hall, Detroit's Orchestra Hall, and at the Phillips Collection in Washington, D.C. Mr. Neubauer's upcoming engagements include performances with the St. Louis Symphony, the North Carolina Symphony, and a recital in New York's Alice Tully Hall. This past summer, he was heard at the Marlboro and Chautauqua Festivals.

Mr. Neubauer began playing the viola at the age of seven. He continued his studies with Alan de Veritch, the late William Primrose, and with Paul Doktor at The Juilliard School. Mr. Neubauer is sponsored by a continuing scholarship from the Epstein Fine Arts Fund of the Boys Clubs of America Young Artists Program, and a Solo Recitalist's Fellowship from the National Endowment for the Arts.

PROGRAM

Paul Neubauer, *viola*   Margo Garrett, *piano*

with Wendy Young, *harpsichord*

Sonata for Viola and Harpsichord	Wilhelm Friedemann Bach
Sonata for Viola and Piano (New York Premiere)	Arthur Foote
Sonata for Unaccompanied Viola, Op. 25, no. 1	Paul Hindemith
Romance Op. 85	Max Bruch
Hejre Kati	Jenö Hubay

All Tickets $6.00/Students and Senior Citizens $3.00
TDF Vouchers
Tickets at Alice Tully Hall Box Office
on day of concert
or mail order to:
The Walter W. Naumburg Foundation.

The Walter W. Naumburg Foundation
144 West 66th Street, New York, N.Y. 10023
(212) 874-1150

THEA DISPEKER Artists' Representative
Patricia A. Winter
Elizabeth Roberts
248 East 78th Street
New York, NY 10021
212/535-1300

photography: Ken Howard
graphic design: Muffet Jones

PAUL NEUBAUER ANALYSIS

The two sides of this concert flyer are stylish and impressive. Its Post-Modern design places the cover photo on the diagonal and plays it against an invisible grid of horizontal and vertical lines. This has the visual effect of pushing the photo to the front and lending it an active, anticipatory quality. You sense the concerto's about to begin.

The gray drop-shadow which partially outlines the photo also seems to push it to a closer plane. If you look closely, you'll see that the type and image elements appear to be layered planes in space moving forward. The black background is as far back as the eye can go, the name of the artist is tucked slightly under the photo and the "Special Award 1982 Viola Competition" is closest to the onlooker—dimensions through design!

The "cover" of the flyer is so good you want to know more. The other side, while unified in concept with the front, adds the *human* dimension with a photo that's a charmer! The drop-shadow behind the picture gives the playful impression that the photo has shifted off the page leaving its shadow behind. The kitten's eyes direct you right into the copy matter which, in my opinion, is just the right length. I think the idea of letting Paul's name function as a headline and the beginning of the copy is a special touch. The comma finds you in the middle of a sentence and you simply must read on. The two horizontal bars isolate the sections of the page so the eye can read down, rest, and *digest*. It is very clean and organized.

I applaud the outstanding design execution of Muffet Jones for the Naumburg Foundation and the imaginative pictures by Ken Howard.

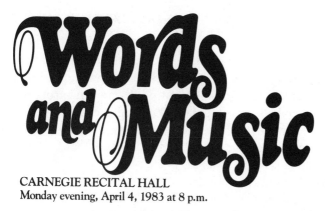

Words and Music

CARNEGIE RECITAL HALL
Monday evening, April 4, 1983 at 8 p.m.

BACA ENSEMBLE

Lucy Rowan, narrator
Robert Mann, Nicholas Mann, violins;
Maureen Gallagher, viola;
Bonnie Hampton, cello
Nathan Schwartz, piano

The photo by Charles Abbott and the design by Muffet Jones convey an impression of casual humor and whimsy. It's fun!

BUT WHAT IF I CAN'T AFFORD A BROCHURE RIGHT NOW?

I'm very glad you asked this question. I'd like to tell you about another presentation format that makes a fine impression, can be updated and adapted for different uses, and doesn't cost a lot. It's my version of a press kit and it's designed to be sent to a potential manager, concert presenter, or media person. I'll explain how I assembled mine, but use this to branch off and suit your own particular needs. This format is not for a broad mailing, however, because it is too costly to post.

First, I purchased boxes of pocket portfolios. These are report covers with two pockets inside, left and right. I chose a gray folder, but they are available in quite a few colors. Then, I asked my printer to letterpress the logo of my ensemble in black ink. I specified its placement in the line of golden proportion. This establishes that a single unit within an area is best displayed on a horizontal plane three-eights of the whole height from the top. Don't let this mathematical jargon deter you, just understand that if you center your name in the middle of the folder, it will optically appear to be sinking toward the bottom quadrant of the page. Thus, it should be placed approximately three to four inches from the top.

Note: An attractive label or flyer could also identify the outside of your folder.

In the inside right pocket, I placed 8x10 photographs, one to three different shots, depending on what I had. In the inside left pocket, I placed 8½x11-inch sheets in the following order:

1. A four-paragraph introduction/description of the ensemble written in a warm, personal style.

2. A sheet that was headed by a bold, italicized quote from a review, a listing of our recent appearances, and the bios of the ensemble members.

3. A sheet that was headed "The United Nations Concert" and gave the program underneath.

4. A reprint of a magazine article about the ensemble.

I did have everything typeset and offset, but if you don't wish to go to that expense, type everything on a good, sharp typewriter (or pay a professional to do it) and find the best photocopy equipment in town. You're still going to get a polished look.

Now, you can add photocopies of reviews, publicity, calendars of this season's appearances, opera/oratorio/orchestral repertoire listings, postcards for demo cassettes, (I'll explain this in the next chapter), or program biographies for use in concert and recital programs—but only include the most important and impressive items or graphics. Keep the number of pages to a minimum to encourage someone to read about you.

I like this format, because it's so fluid. You can add, delete, and keep things current. Plus, your materials stay together on desks with your name prominently displayed.

Mail your packet in an 11½x14½-inch envelope marked "First Class"—and warn the postman on the front and back, "PHOTOS—DO NOT BEND!"

AND DON'T OVERLOOK THESE ECONOMICAL OPTIONS FOR SMALL JOBS

Let's say you are doing a noontime concert and wish to send out a postcard or announcement mailing. The purpose is to get an audience of friends and let people know that you are working—all on a small, friendly scale. There are several inexpensive ways that you could "set the type" yourself and make a simple mechanical. Your neighborhood photocopy center could duplicate and cut it for you.

If there is very little copy, you could go several ways. Let's assume you (or your friend) have an attractive handwriting or a knowledge of calligraphy. You could simply write out the message and achieve a personal, individual look. The text could then be photocopied onto card stock and cut into postcard size. You affix the stamp and mailing label, and voilà! Or you could purchase a Letraset or Prestype alphabet at any art supply store (some stationery stores stock them) and burnish the letters onto paper. How about simply typing out your copy using a good, sharp typewriter? If you mix this type with Letraset for a bold headline, you might come up with an interesting, effective piece. If you can't space well with burnished letters, consider having your headlines typeset professionally. It won't cost all that much, but it will look so much better. Don't forget, you can enlarge or reduce type at a photocopy center.

Of course, there are certain techniques you should know in order to execute these mechanicals, and it would certainly be worthwhile to take a short adult education course to learn the basics of simple mechanical paste-ups. Using these techniques saves you money and gives you the satisfaction of doing it yourself.

Historic St. Paul's Chapel presents

Lise Messier
Soprano

Glenn Parker
Piano

Monday, September 12, 1983   at 12:10 p.m.

Broadway and Fulton Streets
New York City

This is a combination of a typewriter and Prestype (a brand of transfer type). Transfer type is available at any art supply store and at quite a few stationery stores. It comes on sheets, in numerous typefaces and point sizes, and you burnish the letters onto the paper.

Come join me for Sunday BRUNCH at the NEW DEAL in Soho. As the Chef serves delicacies pleasing to your palate, I'll play delicacies pleasing to your ear.

ALAN de MAUSE
SOLO GUITAR 12:00~4:00
Sundays at the NEW DEAL
152 Spring St. 431~3663

This announcement effectively combined Alan's knowledge of calligraphy and the line drawing a friend sketched of him. Even if your friends aren't handy with a pen and ink, you could still incorporate graphic materials in your piece by investigating copyright-free art (also called clip art). Check out the Dover Publications catalog. You find these at most art stores and they contain illustrations on many subjects—including music. Also, check your public library. Many of them maintain extensive clipping files of artwork and illustrations, all of it in the public domain, at no charge.

You are cordially invited to attend
a recital by

Jean Marie Regan, Soprano

Glenn Parker, Piano

Sunday, October 16, 1983
at 4:00 p.m.

Trinity School
91st Street & Columbus Avenue
New York City

R.S.V.P.— (212) 594-3950

This is a nicely worded invitation which was set on a phototypesetting machine. The first line is set in Souvenir Light Italic—14 points. The names and instruments are set in Souvenir Bold Roman—also 14 points—and the remaining is set in Souvenir Light Italic—12 points.

YOU AND THE U.S. POSTAL SERVICE

Now that you've got a few thousand flyers just waiting to get out there and communicate for you, we'd best discuss your options in the mailing department.

Of course first class mail is the only way to ensure the arrival of the piece within a few days. However, a large mailing sent first class would be very expensive. You can save a significant amount of money if you mail third class, bulk rate. As I write, a commercial bulk rate is eleven cents a piece. If your organization is nonprofit, you can qualify for a special bulk rate fee of 5.2 cents a piece. First understand that there are quite a few regulations governing a mailing of this type and, once mailed in this manner, your flyer may take from two to four weeks to arrive. Also, none of the pieces will be returned to you unless you print "address correction requested" under the return address. Then, for twenty-five cents a piece you can see how many flyers had incorrect, out-of-date addresses.

If you decide to mail at the bulk rate, go to the main post office for a permit application. If you want to qualify for the special bulk rate as a not-for-profit organization, you'll need to bring along your federal income tax exemption, certificate of incorporation, a sample mailing and some literature describing the activities of your organization. At any rate, both types of bulk rate mailers must pay a $40.00 annual fee and a one-time, initial fee of $40.00 for the permit number. Note: If you live in a rural area, the local post office will have the application and handle your mailing.

Here's how the system works. Once the post office accepts your application to mail at the bulk rate fee, it assigns a permit number to you and opens a permit account for you at the post office most convenient for your mailing. You cannot bring your mailing to any other branch in the city. Before you haul anything off to that branch, however, you calculate the cost of this particular mailing and bring a check to the main post office of the city you're in. Postage for each mailing is charged to this permit account.

Your printer will have to be instructed to print the permit information on the flyer or envelope in place of a stamp. This is called the *Bulk Rate Indicia*. The copy is a five-line format that looks like this:

Bulk Rate
US Postage
Paid
New York, NY
Permit No. xxxx

When you apply for your permit number and/or pay in advance for each mailing, you will be given forms to fill out regarding each specific mailing, instructions on how to prepare the mailing, and labels to mark them with.

Here's a brief summary to keep in mind:

- The minimum number of pieces in a mailing is 200.

- Flyers must be at least 3½x5 inches with at least 3½x4 inches clear for the address. The fold must be at the top (it's preferable that the piece be machine folded).

- Flyers must weigh less than 3.9111 ounces and be less than ¼ inch thick.

- Very pale or brilliantly colored ink should not be used for the printing of the logo, indicia, or address. Also, too brilliantly colored paper should be avoided. If there's a legibility problem, the entire mailing may be rejected. If you're not sure, bring a sample to the post office for approval.

- The return address of the organization or person who holds the permit must be printed in the left-hand corner, parallel to the length of the brochure or be very prominent inside the mailer.

Now, once you affix address labels, there's quite a production to the next part of the bulk rate mailing procedure. (It's true when they say there's no free lunch.)

The post office requires that you sort the entire mailing according to ZIP code order, bundle the mailing according to category, and secure the bundles by width and girth with sturdy rubber bands. There are four categories of bundles, and you handle the process as follows:

1. First, bundle together all pieces with the same ZIP codes. There *must* be a minimum of ten pieces in each bundle, but a bundle cannot be more than four inches thick. Then, affix in the lower left-hand corner a *red* post office sticker marked "D" for *Direct* on the top piece of each of these bundles. "Direct" bundles go directly from post office of origin to the post office of destination.

2. Now, check the remainder of your mailing to see if you have ten or more pieces with the same first three digits in the ZIP code. Bundle these together and affix a *green* post office sticker marked "3."

3. Look at what's left and see if you have ten or more for the same

state. Bundle these and mark them with the *orange "S"* sticker.

4. There should now be fewer than ten pieces for any given state. Put the remaining pieces in one bundle and write out a slip of paper entitled *"Mixed States"* and tuck it under the rubber bands. (It makes you wonder why the mixed states are left to languish without their own sticker.)

Once you've done the bundling, you place the mailing in sacks given to you by the post office, label the sacks according to post office instructions, and bring them over to the branch to which you were assigned. You turn them in with the proper forms stating the weight and number of pieces.

IMPORTANT! If you make even one error in this sorting process, the post office can call you up, tell you to come and pick up the mailing and redo it, or offer you the option of paying first class postage fees for the estimated percentage of errors in the mailing.

Lest you want to look like Santa Claus dragging sacks across town, you should do the mailing very carefully, *or* pay a mailing house to do it, *or* contact Computers for the Arts and take advantage of their ingenious systems. (See Appendices.)

Two more things: If you write a message on any piece, it becomes first class mail; and, should you wish to mail extra flyers first class, block out the indicia by covering it with a stamp.

CHAPTER 7

Tape It from the Top: Audio and Video Demo Cassettes

I USED TO ENVY MUSICIANS who spent a lot of time in the recording studio. They didn't have to deal with the unsettling one-chance situation of the live performance. If a mistake was made, they simply did it over until it was right, and those magicians known as studio engineers could edit and splice and fatten the sound, and the world could hear captured-forever perfection.

Well, that fantasy came to a rude end the first time I walked into a studio to record. Without an audience it was harder to give a performance and too easy to obsess over every detail. Turning my head to avoid breathing into the microphone was a real adjustment, and my whistling s's drove me crazy. Actually, I was a bit thrown by the experience. Recording is extremely challenging and exacting.

Sooner or later you'll have to cope with the complexities of the situation because contests and competitions, management, concert presenters, and conductors will want to hear you via a demo cassette. Your first recording experience will be full of surprises and revelations, but an understanding of and preparation for the process will help you handle any situation with equanimity.

BOOKING THE SESSION

First, determine what it is you want this tape to achieve. Is it an advertisement for your technique or your beautiful tone? How long will the cassette be? I advise keeping it short, ten to fifteen minutes, unless you are otherwise instructed. Once you are certain of the strengths you wish to display, pick the repertoire which will demonstrate them. Your cassette will reflect these merchandising decisions and make a stronger statement.

It's essential to find the right recording engineer, and it *must* be a person who knows how to record the classical musician. Your engineer has to understand all the instruments and their assorted problems and how to record them with a concert hall realism—a sound with some "space." A rock or pop engineer is after a totally different effect.

Listen to the demo cassettes of other musicians and, if you like the sound, question the musician about the personality of the engineer. Was he or she sympathetic as well as professional? Believe me, it's important. If the answer is yes, get the name and phone number of the engineer.

Find out the studio rates. They usually break down into:

1. An hourly rate (set-up, recording, and editing)

2. Tape charges

3. Copy charges (some studios have copying facilities)

Now, the time-honored rule of thumb is *ONE HOUR FOR ONE MINUTE*. This means that, for every minute of finished product, it takes one hour of set-up, recording, and editing time. Don't assume you are going to beat this formula and save money, so wait until you can comfortably afford the necessary amount of time before booking a session.

When you talk to the engineer, find out exactly what he can do for you. How much time does he think it will take? If you are a pianist, or if the piano is to be included in your instrumentation, find out what kind of piano the studio has. Is it tuned before each session? You should arrange to try it out before you make an appointment. Also, find out if the engineer is flexible. If you have a certain amount of knowledge about yourself in a studio and you want to be miked in a certain way, see if the engineer is willing to try it. Don't forget, though, the engineer knows his own room and mikes and may have to achieve the sound differently. Two open and flexible people will make better music together.

If you decide to make an appointment, find out if there's an hour buffer after the supposed end of your session. You won't be able to come back into the studio and reproduce the same sound in the same situation, so, ensure the proper completion of your tape by giving yourself the option of buying that extra hour.

Important! Find out if the studio is clocking you while you get your sound. Are you being charged to set up and test until everyone is happy with the way he's miked and sounds? Most studios do charge for this.

ADVANCE PREPARATION

All right. You've booked a session, say three weeks from now. Give yourself the time to prepare. You have a lot of homework to do in order to make a smooth, less anxious and less expensive time of it.

You will need to line up your own assisting entourage:

A PRODUCER: by far your *most* important person. The producer should know your sound intimately. He or she will sit in the control booth with the engineer and tell him when he's got it. This way, you don't have to record and waste tape, and then keep running back and forth to the booth to listen. This wastes time (and thus money) and your valuable energy. Also, an artist probably doesn't know his own sound as an audience hears it, so the producer's ears are critical.

The producer can be your spouse or teacher or coach; as long as he or she can read music and understands your sound and the music you'll be recording. Later I'll discuss the way the producer will indicate edits to the engineer.

A PAGE TURNER. Practice with your page turner at home so he or she *slowly* and *quietly* turns pages.

A PIANO TUNER. If you're a real perfectionist, persuade a piano tuner friend to come along and check and recheck the instrument throughout the session.

You've lined up your session and the personnel who will help make it successful. Now I'd like you to read a list of preparations that will help make you ready and relaxed.

1. Memorize as much of the music as possible.

2. Practice playing into a tape recorder with a mike at home. Listen to and for breathing, tone quality and page turns. Check your pitch and timing. Watch the long notes and rests—an anxious musician has a tendency to jump them. Singers, understand that you can't clear your throat or take big breaths into a mike. A lot of recording artists turn their heads away from the mike before they take a good breath. Notate the areas in your music where you'll really need to fill up, and practice into the body the coordination it will take to do this without unbalancing yourself. Also, watch (my downfall) the *hissssing* s's. Pianists, if you like to sing, hum, or breathe along with your music, eliminate these habits before you go into the studio. Instrumentalists, you cannot test the intonation of the note before playing.

   It's time for a little chat. You see, gestures, rapport, facial expressions, and smiles all enhance the live-performance situation and seem to help color a piece. But these elements are lost in the recording studio—it's the music and *nothing else!* Interpretation, mood, and coloration can be conveyed only aurally, so check with your cassette at home and see what's really coming through.

Each instrumentalist will face certain trade-offs between definition and mechanical noise. While these mechanical sounds are imperceptible to the concert hall audience, the "ears" of the mike will pick them up and amplify them for all to hear. Guitarists are often anguished at the squeaking of strings, trumpet players have valve noise problems and flutists will hear key noise (to list a few). Try to minimize the mechanical sounds or decide to go for definition and make a peace with them.

Now let's get back to our list of preparations.

3. If there are tempo changes in the piece or pieces, check the metronomic markings at home and notate them. Take a metronome to the studio (where you'll no doubt be speeding) and check that you are starting the piece at the tempo you decided upon and that you are consistent throughout. If you listen back to a section in the studio, you can set the metronomic marking and pick up at the same tempo when the tape begins to roll again.

4. Photocopy your music and tape it together so there are no unnecessary page turns.

5. Gather together some well-recorded tapes or disc examples of your instrument. Take them to the studio and let the engineer listen to them. He will probably be able to determine how the sound was technically achieved (through the type, position, and distance of mikes and the amount of reverb) and try to achieve the same effect.

6. Make a list of everything you will need with you at the studio. This might include:

   • Two copies of each piece of music—one for you and each instrumentalist and one for the producer.

   • A tuning fork or electronic tuner to check pitch.

   • A metronome.

   • Extra sets of strings, reeds, etc.

- Tapes or discs to demonstrate the recorded sound you like.

One more thing to practice—it's a well-known fact that solo artists listen only to themselves. If you are responsible for the tape, you *must* train yourself to listen critically to all the other players also. Listen up and around at the rehearsals, recording session and editing session.

So, make your transportation plans, confirm the schedule with your assistants *and* the studio engineer, pack up the items you'll be taking along, and get a good night's sleep. Try not to worry. If you've carefully attended to the preparations mentioned above and you've set your awareness, you've greatly reduced the problems that can occur and cause upset.

AT THE STUDIO

You and the people assisting you should arrive thirty minutes earlier than the starting time of your session. If you are nervous, it's understandable; you are looking for perfection and racing against the clock. There will be no audience to cheer you on and inspire you. (I often try to imagine one in order to bring more life to my performance.) The positive aspect here is that you'll get several chances to shoot for perfection.

One small suggestion—watch the amount of coffee you drink before and during the session. You will probably tend to rush, so caffeine won't help matters.

The engineer will begin to place you and your mike. Eye contact is very important between all players, so, if baffles are used for acoustical reasons, let's hope they have windows or that mirrors can be set up so you can see each other. Of course, a classical recording engineer would understand this.

Then the engineer will begin to get sound levels for each instrument. Your producer will talk with him and let him know when he's got the right sound.

Most classical musicians record live to two tracks. This means that as it plays, it is. The balance and blend come from the set-up in the room. You will be recorded at 15 I.P.S. (inches per second) on 1/2-track stereo. This can be copied down to the required specifications. If this tape is for a competition, check the specifications very carefully and bring them in printed form to the engineer to be sure they are fulfilled. Also, ask the engineer to record the session on cassettes as it happens. You can then bring these home, listen to them in a quiet moment and map out for the editor which takes you like best.

As the tape begins to roll, the engineer slates each take sequentially—Take 1, Take 2, and so on. The most efficient way to handle this kind of demo tape session is to divide the musical piece in sections and do one section at a time, re-doing as you go along. This preserves a continuity of sound (particularly for singers whose voices will be different at the beginning and end of the session).

Every time the producer hears an error, he or she will mark the measure with the take number and a minus. The session will not be finished until there is a take number and plus sign over every measure originally marked with a minus.

Note: All the out-takes will be kept on a separate reel. You never know when they might have to be used.

Although they are not always used in the recording of a classical demo tape, I want to mention the use of headphones. You see, the first time I recorded a movie sound track, I hadn't the slightest idea what one did with them! I sort of watched from the corner of my eye and did my best to look nonchalant. I want you to have more savvy in the studio. Headphones are used when:

1. You are singing or playing to prerecorded music on another track. You listen and record along. There may be a click track fed in through the headphones to give you the metronomic tempo of the prerecorded sequences.

2. The engineer, for acoustical reasons, needs a separation between instruments. One instrumentalist may be isolated in a booth and the only way one can hear the other is through headphones.

3. It is sometimes possible to have a cue mix pumped through the "cans." This is the sound precisely as you would like to hear it while performing (though not as it's actually being recorded)—i.e., more of you, more of another instrument. Some reverb on your sound can boost your confidence.

EDITING, DUPLICATION, DISTRIBUTION

After your recording session, go home and relax. Don't attempt to listen to the cassettes until you are rested and refreshed; when you are, listen intellectually and make notations of the takes that please you. Take these notes and tapes with you to your editing session. There, you'll sit with the editor, discuss the edits and listen to what he does. The corrections that were marked with a plus sign the day of the recording are called *inserts*.

EXAMPLE

Let's assume that take 3 is the basic complete take for this piece. However, there were two errors—in measure 2 and measure 11. The producer indicated these problems with a minus sign and the take number over the measure in question. The producer later noted that these measures were well-played in takes 7 and 9 (in the case of measure 2), and in take 9 (in the case of measure 11). He then placed a plus sign before these take numbers over these measures. If the playing were of high quality in take 9, the editor would no doubt choose to insert take 9 because it would cover measures 2-11 and reduce the number of edits. Note: This is harder to describe and read through than it is to actually notate in the studio. Don't let this scare you!

These inserts are inaudibly spliced into a *master* tape and then a 15 I.P.S. copy is made. This copy, called the *safety*, is used to make duplications.

Ask the studio how much they would charge to duplicate the tape for you. If you need a significant number of cassettes, there are high-speed duplication businesses who do this. Ask the engineer or editor to recommend a firm that does a lot of classical demo duplication, or look in the Yellow Pages under Recording-High-Speed Cassette Duplication. Most of these companies will type and affix labels and supply cases for a modest price. Make sure you identify the case of the cassette also. Type out the names of the performers and pieces and indicate the overall length of the demo.

It is crucial that you listen to every cassette all the way through before sending it to anyone. In my enthusiasm to mail one off to a friend in Oklahoma, I failed to take the time to do this check. She gathered half her friends and university colleagues together and they all got to listen to me sounding like something straight out of *The Exorcist!*

Mail the cassettes in a padded mailing envelope, first class. Mark the dates and programs on the boxes of your master and safety tapes and store them in a cool place away from speakers or magnets.

As you'll soon find out, cassettes are not inexpensive, and you'll want to distribute them judiciously. I made up a self-addressed postcard and enclosed it with my brochure. (See the illustrations on the next page.) Anyone really interested in listening could fill out the postcard, drop it in the mail, and receive a cassette by return mail. My activity chart revealed a substantial number of requests, so this system worked for me.

A final note. If you have an excellent recording of a live performance, you might want to use it and bypass the expenses of the studio. However, if the audience was small and the applause not too beefy, take the tape to an engineer and have him either cut out the applause entirely, or turn the volume down after the first audible clap. (You'll look too modest for words.) Paltry applause after a terrific performance absolutely levels the professional impression and is a real letdown for the listener.

SO YOU WANT TO BE IN PICTURES

For years, an artist attracted attention through the use of brochures, head shots, publicity, live performance, and recording. Now technology has brought us a new way to represent ourselves: the video cassette. This is an exciting development that you can use to command attention and impress the viewer in an entertaining manner.

Video is becoming more and more important as an audition format, also. The prohibitive expense of transportation today makes it impractical for an artist or ensemble to widen an audition circuit. A video cassette, though, could wing its way to a prospective presenter for the price of postage and still give a very live impression of your artistic presence.

Should you decide to present yourself in living color, the following discussion will help you sort things out.

First of all, there are three formats used in video (format refers to the size of tape—the more bits of information that can be put in an area, the better the picture):

½″—VHS and Beta—home video systems

stamp

A Small Circle Of Friends

37 W. Author's Avenue
New York, New York
10023

Dear Friends,

Yes, we would like to hear your demo tape. Please send it by return mail to:

Name: _____

Address: _____

_____ Phone:_____

3/4"—Industrial and broadcast use
(recommended for demo cassette)
1"—Used by TV stations for broadcasting

A musician's demo should be shot in 3/4". This can then be dubbed down to 1/2" VHS or Beta if necessary. A good "wardrobe" of cassettes would consist of three 3/4" and three 1/2".

FINDING A PRODUCER

The person you need to locate to execute this project is called a *producer.* You find one either by word of mouth or by looking in the trade papers (e.g., *Back Stage* or *Variety).* Because this is a relatively new option for musicians, you will have a lot of research to do in order to ensure your getting a reputable producer and a good-looking cassette.

The charges will probably break down this way:

1. An hourly rate (no doubt a four-hour minimum)

2. Tape costs

3. Editing (charged per hour—an uncomplicated job may take two to four hours)

Some producers will offer you a package that includes the consultation, filming, tape, and editing, and an additional charge for duplication. Get several quotes from recommended producers and sit down and figure it all out, *but first* find out the level of the camera and recording equipment. There are three:

Home commercial

Industry quality

Broadcast quality

The level you need is industrial or broadcast and when you're doing your research on the phone, make certain this is what the producer will use. Also, make an appointment to review a bit of the work done by this person with his equipment so you can judge the quality of the imagery and sound. If a producer balks at this, be leery.

If everything seems to check out positively, begin to discuss your needs, market, and budget. You don't want to be talked into anything you don't need and can't afford. The finished demo should be on the short side and it should be upbeat and interesting but not too jazzy. The tape should complement you and your talent, not vice versa. Remember: you are not the icing on the cake; you *are* the cake! Tell your producer this is in essence an audition, not an advertising overkill.

The producer, on this level, is the person who puts everything together. He consults, he develops the concept, and he directs the lighting, the sound, the filming, and the editing. In short, the producer is responsible for the entire production.

THE SHOOT

Now, depending on how you want to emphasize or enhance your material, the shoot could be handled several ways:

1. Filming during a live performance, also known as *documentation* or *real time.*

2. Simulating a performance by renting a theatre or studio and using lights and a thunderous (naturally) applause track.

3. Performing in the park, on the street, on the steps of a historic or picturesque building, on the harbor, on the Golden Gate Bridge, etc. You might need a shooting permit from the city to do this, and the soundtrack would have to be prerecorded due to street noise.

The financial terms which will put this project in action are probably a 50 percent deposit before the shoot, the remaining amount due upon completion. It's a good idea to ask for a typed confirmation of all services, number of cassettes, prices, location, date and time of shoot, plus an indication of the deposit paid. Because a project like this can run over budget, ask the producer to include a clause that stipulates that the price may not fluctuate more than 10 percent over agreed upon costs.

Prepare for your shoot by notating the metronomic markings and taking a metronome with you to begin the piece at the tempo previously decided upon.

Also, ask your producer for a makeup and wardrobe consultation. No doubt, you'll be told to keep the makeup natural and that you cannot wear large stripes or dots. They distract from the presentation because stripes on video strobe, or appear to be moving, and dots bleed. Show your producer what you plan to wear and discuss the mood you wish to convey. He can gel the lights to help achieve a unified look to the production. For instance, a blue wash might give the production a ballad-like mood, etc.

Of course the producer will have to hear a tape recording of the pieces you plan to present. From this he will develop the concept, the *storyboard*, and the *shooting script*. The storyboard is a cartoon sketch of every angle and shot the producer plans to capture on film and the shooting script is the outline of these technical shots.

I think there should definitely be titles and credits—it's an impressive way to register your name in the viewer's mind—just keep them short.

Let me demonstrate the hypothetical agenda of a solo pianist's shoot and edit with one camera. This will give you an idea of the process and vocabulary.

First, the producer will take an *establishing shot*. This establishes who, where, and what for the viewer. So, we see John Smith from a distance, sitting at the piano and playing. The entire piece would be played, recorded, and filmed straight on from this focal point. If mistakes are made, the pianist backs up to a place before the error and goes on from there.

Then, in order to film *inserts,* the visual pictures laid over the existing audio track, the producer would change the camera angle and shoot a tight shot of the hands on the keyboard. The pianist might wear earphones and listen to that particular passage in order to coordinate the movement of his fingers with the timing at which he originally recorded. Once more the camera would be moved, and close-ups of the face filmed. Of course, three cameras could accomplish this quickly, but the fees for staff and equipment would go beyond the pocketbooks of most artists.

These changes of perspective will be cut to and from the establishing shot in the editing room and will give the demo cassette visual variety, interest, and rhythm.

CAN IT

Once everything is in the "can," the film is edited. Here, the producer contemplates the pacing. The principle of this is to start on one level, build on previous information, build to a climax, and resolve. You build by upping the tempo of the cuts. This cutting back and forth adds a dynamic dimension to the music and the artist. Ah, the magic of movies!

The editing process will also create the *lead in* and *lead out* of the demo. That is, getting from a blank screen into the production (or up to the light source) and fading out or going black at the end. The titles and credits will be added during editing.

Depending on how much enthusiasm and excitement you want to inspire, an applause track can be added to the audio. Don't laugh, it does inspire the viewer's level of appreciation.

Once you get your cassettes, mark them and their cases explicitly and store them in a cool (heat stretches tape), dry place away from speakers or magnets.

Two more recommendations. Mail your cassette in a padded mailing bag marked *Fragile* and don't forget to insure it!

Also, keep a record of where each one went and when. You must make the viewer understand the tape's value so you'll get it back within a decent interval. Consider sending along a stamped, self-addressed mailer. And I think it's a good idea to complement your tape with an accompanying graphic presentation such as a press book. This can be a simple folder with inside pockets into which you place some biographical information (brochures, pictures, etc.) and something about the program the viewer is about to watch.

CHAPTER 8

Management—Who Needs It?

THE VERY WORD *management* is guaranteed to provoke extreme reactions in musicians. Some become confused and disoriented; others react with bulging eyes and a sharp intake of breath, closely followed by the spitting out of the latest horror story. Examining the rosters listed in the *Musical America Directory* year to year is like watching some fascinating game of musical chairs, there's so much hopping about. An understanding of the realities of the situation would do much, I'm convinced, to straighten out the problem and protect you from those few unscrupulous managers.

Some artists see management as a return to the breast—the manager will take care of them, nurture them, move mountains for them. But if you want your mom, call home, not your manager. He or she is trying to survive in this business, just as you are. As in a good marriage, you are partners, both working hard and, ideally, in concert. The following discussion should demystify this subject.

Q: When am I ready for management?
A: When you are marketable—when you are commanding fees that would interest a manager netting 20 percent. All management firms are businesses and every artist on the roster counts. Normally, you should have a substantial number of reviews from reputable newspapers that, for the most part, exclaim the same virtues. If you are an ensemble, the manager will want to know that you, as a group, work and travel well together and exhibit an ease with each other on stage. Your repertoire must be varied, and you must have the financial stability to enter into a contrac-

tual agreement with the firm (more about this later). Of course, an extraordinary talent and a big prize winner will come to the attention of management more easily than most.

Q: Should I seek large or small management?

A: It depends. Some large, established firms may spend more time dealing with requests for their more stellar talents. A small company *may* be more aggressive, more interested in nurturing a young talent. The newer manager may simply be less tired than his more experienced colleague who has battled the profession for years. However, a newer, smaller management may not have the contacts or reputation to get you engagements.

Q: Will a manager be interested in me if I live in Vermont? Must I move to New York?

A: Your home base may be anywhere in the country as long as you're willing to travel to fulfill engagements. Granted, the majority of large management firms are in New York City, but many of the artists on their rosters have positions at universities or residencies all over the country. Musicians are a mobile bunch. You know, there *are* managers on the West Coast and in varous regions of the United States.

Q: How will I know which management to approach?

A: Do your homework! Consult *The Musical America Directory* to start with—most libraries have this invaluable reference book which includes descriptions of managements as well as their rosters. Don't approach a management that already represents your category of musician abundantly. A conflict of interests would arise, and it would be a signal that you (and the management that might consider you) are indiscriminate. Seek instead a firm that could use your talents to balance its roster, and then find out as much as you can about its reputation. You might want to call a few people listed on the roster and ask for an honest assessment.

Q: When and how do I approach a management firm?

A: When you have specific and discerning reasons for contacting an agency, do so. The letter you write—perhaps the first impression they will have of you—is extremely important. Never send a form letter! Write a letter that is professional, specific, and convincing. Tell the management firm why you are approaching *them* in particular as well as why you think you are marketable, but don't hit them over the head with what a genius you are.

Delos String Quartet

Music Department
The University of Delaware
Newark, Delaware 19711
(302) 738-2577

8 May 1981

Mr. Charles Hamlen and Ms. Edna Landau
Hamlen/Landau Management, Inc.
Suite 2A, 140 W. 79 Street
New York, New York 10024

Dear Mr. Hamlen and Ms. Landau:

We met once, briefly, after a concert the New World String Quartet gave in Philadelphia at the Performing Arts Series.

Today, I am writing to tell you that the Delos String Quartet (whose violist I am) won First Prize with "unanimity and congratulations" of the international jury at the 14th International String Quartet Competition in Colmar, France. There was no second prize awarded.

The quartet has also completed a very successful first European tour this January and February (excerpts of reviews enclosed).

We would like to ask you whether you would be interested in taking on the U.S. management of the Delos Quartet. After talking to members of the New World Quartet, we were very impressed with what you had done for them. Their comments prompted us to write to you in particular.

I am including some materials about the quartet. If you need anything else, I can be reached at the number listed above. I do hope we get a chance to speak soon.

Thank you for your attention.

Yours sincerely,

Barbara Westphal

Barbara Westphal
for
The Delos Quartet

The management firm was impressed with this letter. It made the connection in the first paragraph, it was to the point, specific, and didn't hit them over the head. The letter presented the musicians warmly and professionally.

It piqued the interest of the readers and gave them all the information simply and quickly.

Q: What else should I include with the letter?
A: Be sure to include several of your reviews, and by all means, excerpt the good parts. Never send the entire review if there are unpleasant remarks mixed in, unless it is requested that you do so. Also, send any good graphic materials. If you send a tape, go to any lengths to make sure it's of the highest quality. (Note: make sure you label the tape, not just the case.) Do not bombard a prospective management with too much material.

Q: What would really turn management off?
A: Bragging that you are the best the world has seen. Interest, equanimity and a modest pride are more appropriate qualities to demonstrate.

Q: If the management firm is interested, what happens?
A: Arrangements will be made for an audition and an interview. If all goes well and feelings are good on both sides, the manager will discuss what he thinks he can do for you and outline what he expects from you professionally and financially.

Q: Let's say a management signs us, what then?
A: Each firm works a bit differently and every detail should be worked out before you sign anything. However, all managers will need to have brochures designed for you (roughly 10,000 copies will be printed), photos must be taken and reproduced and tapes recorded and reproduced. At this writing these "selling aids" will cost approximately:

brochures:	$800-$1,500
photos:	$300-$500
(plus duplications)	
tapes:	$300-$500
(plus duplications)	

These costs are *totally* absorbed by the artist. Then, the artist generally pays for all postage for promotional mailings and correspondence, telephone calls, his share of the yearly *Musical America Directory* ad and any other advertising.

Normally the artist receives a statement every month or two, advising her or him how much she or he owes for that period of time. These monthly fees and the selling aids may add up to over $3,000 for the first year alone, and have nothing to do with the 20 percent commission fee the manager takes when he secures a booking. A manager is not a bank or a parent agreeing to support you. These expenses are incurred on your behalf and are, naturally, yours. This is why a management will want to explore whether or not you are financially responsible.

Some managements require several thousand dollars up front, upon signing the contract (which might run for a two- or three-year period). Some may want a monthly retainer. I don't think this is a good idea, but if you agree to it, *be sure* to ask for a monthly statement in return, advising you what the manager has been doing with that retainer.

Q: What does the manager really do for me? Must I have one?

A: Initially, a manager provides you with more visibility than income. A good manager knows the presenters and those who do the booking and tries to sell your talents to them. Presenters rely heavily on the discriminating taste of management, which is another reason why these firms are so selective about the artists they take on. Apart from negotiating fees and contracts, the management firm handles the logistics of travel tickets, hotel reservations, and car or van rental. The manager also coordinates publicity for the concert and provides the presenter with program details and up-to-date biographies and photographs of the performers. He also follows up to secure reviews after the performance.

Q: How come my brother is an actor signed with the William Morris Agency and he doesn't pay monthly expenses and his commission fee is only 10 percent?

A: Agencies such as these have stars who easily contract for one million dollars. Ten percent of that will pay of lot of overhead! Unfortunately, classical artists (unless you are a Horowitz, Domingo, or Rampal) can expect only a very modest ceiling on fees for any one booking.

Q: Wait a minute, let me do a bit of arithmetic here. Say I'm a member of a string quartet, we do extremely well and we command a $3,000 fee . . . take off 20 percent (or $600)—we're left with $2,400—divided by four— Ah! We each get $600?

A: Yes. Now understand that you are each responsible for your own transportation, hotel bills, and food.

Q: My God! How can we survive?

A: Faith helps. Block booking is another resource. Your manager will try to arrange several concerts in the same area. You pay your expenses, commission, and monthly fee (if there is one) with the first concert, and hopefully make a profit on the others.

Q: You had me nervous there for a minute! Now, how long before it all works out this way?

A: It may take (I think you'd better sit down) three, four, or more years to work up a decent schedule and sustain the activity. Some years, of course, will be better than others. A management may book a few concerts for you in the first year, and then the "Sophomore Slump Syndrome" may strike. You must be prepared to weather the capriciousness of the situation. Some managers will help you develop residencies and master class presentations to supplement your income. A good manager will *try* to nurture your talent, advise you, and help you fulfill your potential, but it takes time!

Q: What would I want to avoid in a manager?

A: One who does not guard your physical and mental health while he races you around to make as much money as possible. Also, do not let anyone push you to do anything you're not ready for (this is a particular problem for young singers). Remember, only you know your own stamina and how much time you require for rest, practice, and proper preparation. *Communicate* with your manager!

Q: All right. If I reach the conclusion that I'm not yet ready for management, what do I do?

A: We're coming full circle here. You can prepare for management (and maybe find out you are your own best manager) by doing the following:

1. Build your repertoire and coach with professionals.

2. Get exposure, experience, and reviews in every conceivable way. Book yourself through friends, universities, organizations, and connections. Get on the telephone and don't give up!

3. Get publicity so that you are "news" (more about that in the next chapter). Competitions offer a lot of exposure even if you don't come out the winner.

4. Contact the management you think you'd like to sign with in the future whenever you are doing something *important*. Let them get to know you over a period of time. You must, in a way, win them over and this could take several "campaigns" over a two-year period. Be positive, but not a pest. One more thing—once you have signed with management, don't assume they go to sleep at night thinking of you. You must stay in touch with them and make yourself visible. It's a well-known fact that people tend to think of those they've recently seen or had contact with. Developing a relationship with your manager and the staff in the office is very important.

With or without a manager, you must pay your dues, put in the time, and do your homework. Persistence, sincerity, enthusiasm, intelligence, and stability, along with a talent that is marketable, will draw the proper attention to you. Having the right manager makes it that much easier.

CHAPTER 9

Spreading the News: You and Your Public

IT'S ONE THING to perfect your skills as a musician and attract attention from concert presenters, conductors, and managers. It's another thing to be introduced to the general public, gain its understanding and acceptance, and arouse in people the desire to hear you more often. Welcome to the greater world of public relations!

Publicity informs and excites the public and sells seats. And a full house makes a concert presenter so happy he will no doubt engage you again, sing your praises to your management, and spread the good news to other presenters. This is the result we are seeking, and your willingness and ability to generate publicity will do a lot to obtain it. Plus, clippings and past media exposure that you can reproduce or mention lend an air of credibility and excitement to you. This merchandising of your publicity will heighten the interest and appreciation level of future presenters or media personnel, so any way you look at it, publicity is a boon.

A publicist is the professional you hire to be your ambassador to the media, but, as we'll later discuss, the fees for this kind of work are substantial. Until you're generating enough income and have reached a certain career level that warrants the hiring of a publicist, you're going to have to handle this job in a basic way yourself. This chapter will introduce you to the various media outlets, their personnel, and the formats with which they deal.

The good news is that there exists an entire communications network which needs ideas and information. Media people have feature columns, review columns, calendar listings, and radio and TV programs to fill with ink and audio/visuals and someone has to tune them into what's going on. They therefore view the publicist (and you, if you're wearing this hat for now) as reporters in the field. It's estimated that over 60 percent of the stories in a daily newspaper are the result of someone contacting the paper on the behalf of the story's subject. If you can write a good press release and calendar listing, think of an interesting angle for a feature story and write an effective "pitch letter," or persuade a producer of a radio or TV program of your value as a guest, you gain a chance at reaching the eyes and ears of the public.

WRITING A PRESS RELEASE

A press release is the announcement of your concert to editors and reviewers. It outlines a news story and provides background information. It's important that the release follow a professional format and it is vital that it capture the attention of the reader quickly. If you have hired a concert manager or publicist to handle your concert, he or she will write and mail the release. If not, the following will show you that it's something you can do yourself once you take the time to study the style and analyze the tone and merchandising technique.

Let's consider the practicalities first:

- Type out the release on white paper, double spaced with ample margins.

- At the top, right-hand corner, put the name of the person to be contacted for additional information. Put that person's telephone number immediately below. This can be a friend or teacher as long as the person is articulate and available.

- A release date goes right below the telephone number. In the case of a musical event, this would invariably read, "FOR IMMEDIATE RELEASE." It's also a good idea to list the day you are sending the release under this.

- Now, center the headline in all capital letters. This is a short phrase which gives the editor an idea what the story is about. The headline should be intriguing and lead the person reading it to move on for more.

- Your text follows.

- Mark the end of the release with this symbol: ###. It's nice to keep the release short and contained on one page, but if you need two pages, mark the end of page 1 with the word "MORE" and mark the next page with an abbreviated headline (called a slug) and identify it as page 2. The release should be 350 words or less.

- You can duplicate your release simply by photocopying it, or having it offset.

EDITORIAL CONSIDERATIONS FOR YOUR TEXT

Because a busy editor may read no further than the lead (or first) paragraph, this all-important paragraph must be specific, concise, and evoke immediate interest. Included should be *the famous five W's:* WHO, WHAT, WHERE, WHEN, and WHY. This means you announce WHO is performing WHAT, WHERE, and WHEN. The "WHY" is the "W" to spend time with. This is your news peg, the reason this performance should command attention. If you are premiering a piece of music, it's the first performance in two hundred years, the concert has a tie-in with an anniversary, or there's something very unusual about the ensemble, you've got a possible "WHY."

All the paragraphs should be written in an inverted pyramid construction. This means that the important facts are first and details follow. Using quotes from some very favorable reviews is an effective way to establish credibility and to persuade the editor that the event is worthy of space in his publication.

The subsequent paragraphs can give descriptions of the performer's background, the ensemble, the repertoire, guest artists, or a recent tour. Follow your instincts about what is important.

The concluding paragraph should list ticket prices and availability, the box office telephone number, hours, and address.

Although your press release should hinge on this format as much as possible, remember there is still room for an individual and enthusiastic voice.

Note: Press releases are usually sent out six weeks prior to an event. Check the deadline requirements for each publication, though. Just call and ask to speak to the music editor.

A LISTING RELEASE

Most newspapers and magazines print listings of daily cultural events, and these calendars are important publicity for your performances. Find out who the calendar editor is for each of the area's publications and send

Contact: Janice Papolos
(212)765-4321
FOR IMMEDIATE RELEASE
March 25, 1983

KAHAN AND BRAHMS AT MERKIN HALL ON MAY 7, 1983

Pianist Sylvia Kahan, celebrating the 150th anniversary of the birth of Johannes Brahms, will make her New York debut at Merkin Concert Hall at the Abraham Goodman House, 129 W. 67th Street at 8:00 p.m. on Saturday, the 7th of May, 1983.

Ms. Kahan has concertized throughout North America and Europe as soloist with orchestra, as well as recitalist and chamber musician. She has been on the artist-faculty at the Delta Festival and the New Mexico Music Festival, where she appeared as soloist for two seasons with the Festival Chamber Orchestra. Her playing has been broadcast on National Public Radio. Recently, she returned from an extensive concert tour of Scandinavia, the British Isles, and Western Europe.

A highly sought-after collaborative artist in New York City, Ms. Kahan has appeared with internationally acclaimed instrumentalists in Alice Tully Hall, Carnegie Recital Hall, and the 92d Street Y. She has accompanied the public master classes of Claus Adam, Doriot Anthony Dwyer, and Joel Krosnick.

Sylvia Kahan holds degrees from the Oberlin Conservatory of Music and Michigan State University. She has studied with such noted pianists as Edith Kraft, Jonathan Feldman, Ralph Votapek, and Jens Nygaard.

The May 7th program will include the Beethoven Sonata in E-flat, Op. 31, no. 3, the Fantasia-Variations of Ben Weber and three short pieces by Fauré and will feature the Sonata in C Major, Op. 1 of Brahms. Ms. Kahan has a particular affinity for this composer. "It was Brahms' piano music that first made me decide to become a pianist," she explained. Later, attending concerts during the Beethoven Bicentennial Year, she felt a strong impulse to celebrate the bicentennial of Brahms: "When I checked the date, I found out it was May 7th of the year 2033. I was crushed, because, by then, I would be eighty and arthritic!" She opted to rejoice in her youth *and* his music and reserved the celebration for Brahms' 150th anniversary instead.

Tickets are available for $6.00 beginning April 15th at Merkin Concert Hall Box Office at 129 West 67th Street in New York City. TDF Vouchers are accepted and students and senior citizens are admitted for $4.00. For inquiries, call the box office from noon to 8:00 p.m. at 212/362-8719. Credit card reservations are accepted—Call Chargit at 212/944-9300.

him or her a release prepared specifically for that kind of listing. Don't send the entire press release and expect the editor to sift out the important facts. Instead, prepare a condensed version of your already written press release (something like the example shown). The information should include a brief who, what, why, when, where, and how much, and where to call for ticket information. Often a program description is printed, so include that in the listing release also.

Check the deadline requirements for each publication. A magazine may need your release more than two months in advance of your program date. A newspaper will have different requirements. Some publications will feature a good photo, so take a chance and send one in.

Contact: Janice Papolos
(212)765-4321
FOR IMMEDIATE RELEASE

KAHAN AND BRAHMS AT MERKIN HALL ON MAY 7, 1983

Pianist Sylvia Kahan, celebrating the 150th anniversary of the birth of Johannes Brahms, will make her New York debut at Merkin Concert Hall at the Abraham Goodman House, 129 W. 67th Street at 8:00 p.m. on Saturday, the 7th of May, 1983. The program will include Beethoven, Fauré, Ben Weber, and the Brahms Sonata in C Major, Op. 1. Tickets are $6.00. For inquiries call: (212)362-8719.

HOW TO GET A FEATURE STORY OR RADIO/TV INTERVIEW

You must begin to develop a nose for news. What's unusual about you or your ensemble? What might be interesting about a tour you're doing or a concert program? Has something very human happened to you in your life or travels as a musician? If you can see why the general public might find that something amusing or moving, you might be able to interest a newspaper or magazine in writing a feature story about you. You also might be able to get an interview on radio or TV. The best way to present or confirm your angle to an editor or program producer is through a pitch letter. This is simply a letter requesting a feature story, editorial support, or an interview. If you, or someone in your organization, has strong writing skills and is willing to write the story from the first-person view, that may increase your chances of getting space and this should be spelled out in the letter.

Because there are so many variables in each situation, it's perhaps best to call first, introduce yourself and gauge interest in the idea. You can be warmer and more immediate on the phone and sometimes, in the process of talking to an editor, the angle clarifies and develops. Then, that day, confirm the conversation and angle via the pitch letter.

The letter should be brief, typed, and *personalized*. This means that it must be geared to the specific interests and needs of the column or program in which you hope to be featured. Thus, you have a lot of research and thinking to do before you make that call or write that letter. It will pay off though, because you won't be wasting anyone's time and you'll be armed with a lot of facts and focus. This will increase the probability of your success. Keep in mind, too, that the Arts section is not the only place to target for possible publicity. Tie-ins may be appropriate in the Food Section, Living Section, etc. Don't limit yourself.

Now, if you are seeking your publicity in print media (newspapers and magazines), and this is the first contact you are making, the opening paragraph should be arresting (even startling) and go on to outline the news peg or angle of a possible article. Some information about your background should be included. Conclude the letter with a phrase that tells the reader you will follow up with a phone call in a week in order to discuss the idea. And, when you do, refer to the letter and remind the editor briefly of its contents. Then, ask if there is any interest in the idea. Ideally, this results in your sitting at the table one morning, drinking coffee and reading the newspaper . . . and . . . wait a minute! . . . THERE YOU ARE!

If you are suggesting a radio or TV interview, make it a point in the letter to mention that the spokesperson or persons are articulate, dynamic, and charming. This must be the case if you wish to garner publicity in these media.

Of course, it is easier (and often more effective) for a third party to make the approach and confirm how deserving you are of recognition. Where that person sounds enthusiastic and objective you would sound like a braggart. Are you beginning to see why a publicist might have a place in your life eventually? Until you are ready for that step, though, you might consider appointing one of your friends or family "official publicist for . . .," or tone down the letter and let quotes from reviews rave about you.

The pitch letters on the following pages will illustrate various angles and situations.

A Note About Photos

Photographs included with your releases, listings, or pitch letters can complement the story and heighten the interest of the editor. A picture really is worth a thousand words, so if you have a good one and it is used, it's wonderful publicity. The photos you send should be 8x10 or 5x7—glossy or matte finish in black and white. There should be sharp contrasts between areas of dark and light and a light background is preferable. Very few publications use color photography, and if they did, they would require slides or transparencies, not color prints.

The photo *must* be captioned. This is really a mini-release (sometimes called a cut-line) which is typed double-spaced on the lower half of a sheet of paper. It is then taped or glued to the back of the photo so the typed caption is visible below. Finally, the paper is folded up over the face of the photo. The copy should give the contact name, number, all relevant information about the event, name of the photographer, and names of the people pictured.

MEET THE PRESS

Now that you understand some of the media contact formats, let's review several of the potential avenues of exposure and how you go about finding them in your community.

MEDIA OUTLETS

Daily and Weekly Newspapers

Local, National, and Special Interest Magazines

Newsletters, Bulletins, and Corporate House Organs

Wire Services*

Radio

Television/Cable

---

*Wire services disseminate stories and pictures to newspapers and stations over a state, regional, or national territory. There are two national wire services: Associated Press (AP) and United Press International (UPI). To find the local wire service contacts look up Associated Press and United Press International in the phone book.

The Doberman Beach Concert Series

2 April 1983

Mr. John Dobbs
Entertainment Editor
The Holmes Star Ledger
3 Mystery Lane
Holmes, California 90068

Dear John:

After our phone conversation yesterday, I thought of an angle that might result in an interesting story vis-à-vis the Garrett Trio debut for us on April 29th.

Mrs. Fancy Schmancy is hosting a lavish dinner party in honor of the trio and the close of our 39th season. The well-known French chef, Pierre Pierre, is preparing several interesting dishes and an interview of him with recipes would be a treat for all area gourmands.

I have spoken to Mrs. Schmancy and Monsieur Pierre and both agree to such a story.

Thanks ever so much for your kind consideration and help in thinking of possible tie-ins. I'll call next week to discuss the idea with you.

Until then, best wishes.

Cordially,

Agatha Greenson

Agatha Greenson
Publicity Chairman

April 30, 1983

Ms. Lucy Riches, Feature Editor
The Philadelphia Courier
30th Street Station
Philadelphia, Pennsylvania 19102

Dear Ms. Riches:

A person who is one of the few well-known male harpists active today, who is a classically trained musician but is considered an expert in the pops field as well, who graduated from Juilliard and was the first American to be a member of the Berlin Philharmonic under Herbert von Karajan but who also played for years at the Warehouse Restaurant/Lounge in Marina Del Rey, Los Angeles, and who was first harpist of the Istanbul Symphony and the Honolulu Symphony (yes, it's all the same person!) will be playing a recital in Philadelphia on June 2. His name is DeWayne Fulton.

I am telling you all this as a way of suggesting that you do a story on him. His story is appealing to many more people than just the classically oriented public because of his involvement with popular music. And his stories are fantastic, telling about everything from working with von Karajan to living in Turkey. If this is not enough, he also had as "regulars" at the Warehouse the likes of John Wayne, Tom Jones, Ava Gardner, Charlton Heston and many others. Plus, he has played for Emperor Hirohito and the Royal Family at the Imperial Palace in Japan, as well as for Presidents Lyndon Johnson and Ronald Reagan—under interesting circumstances!

DeWayne Fulton's "cause" has been to popularize the harp—to bring it before many people—by performing all types of music. As the instrument is usually known only for its presence at the rear of the orchestra, it is most unusual to have one played as a solo instrument. DeWayne, by the way, also performs on the Irish folk harp and uses electronic modification for all sorts of effects.

I will speak with you soon, and hope this story is a possibility.

With all best regards,

Nancy Shear
Publicist

180 WEST END AVENUE/NEW YORK, NY 10023/(212) 595-0793

Paul Bogdasarian

10 SPRAGUE ROAD
NEW CANON, CONNECTICUT 06840
(203) 541-6674

September 27, 1983

Mr. David S. Wright, Program Director
WGCX-FM
42 Eight Avenue
Charleston, South Carolina 29403

Dear Mr. Wright:

On November 31st, I will have the honor of performing with the Charleston Philharmonic. This will be my first time in your city.

As you may know, I have won three major competitions: the Naumburg, Van Cliburn and Arthur Rubinstein. I am a graduate of Indiana University where I studied with Cheryl Gallan for three years.

Not many people understand just what is involved in building a career in music today, or what the life of a professional musician is like (traveling from city to city, learning new compositions while keeping the old repertory fresh, dealing with the constant comi-tragedy of terrible instruments, and so on). Also, my program is an interesting one which has some unusual stories attached to it.

I will be arriving in town on the afternoon of November 29th and would like very much to appear as a guest on your program. A copy of my biography is enclosed for your perusal. I could also supply recordings of my playing for use on the program or, if a good piano is available in the studio, would be happy to perform live on the show.

I look forward to hearing from you and hope that we will be able to meet—on or off the air!

Yours sincerely,

Paul Bogdasarian

Paul Bogdasarian

The Rogeri Trio

Pictured in the snowfall are (left) Carter Brey, cello; (center) Barbara Weintraub, piano; and (right) Richard Young, violin. The trio performs at the Frick Art Museum, 7227 Reynolds Street, Pittsburgh at 3:00 p.m. on February 12, 1984. (Photo by David Herrenbruck.) For further information call: (412)371-7766.

Publicity begins at home, so check out the local media outlets first. Read the papers carefully and tune into the radio and TV stations. Make a note of writers and the angles they continually present. When you're at the supermarket, pick up the weekly "shopper" and scan it for calendar listings or entertainment features. If you are planning a concert that features music from a certain nation, check if there is a newspaper pertaining to that ethnic population. Remember how often you've thrown away your college or professional organization's newsletter or journal? You've been passing up a very possible publicity outlet. Once you change your mindset and begin to think about exposure, you'll be amazed at how many avenues actually exist.

If you are seeking broader coverage, the following list will help you pinpoint media outlets in other states or on a national level, but you really must call the switchboards and verify that the person listed as editor or producer is still working in that capacity.

1. The Yellow Pages is always a good place to start. Look up "Newspapers," "Radio," "Television," and "Wire Services," etc.

2. Look at the back pages of the *Musical America Directory* for a listing of newspapers in each state. Note: this list is not complete.

3. Call the local Arts Council (see Appendices). They often have compiled press lists for their area.

4. Go to the reference room of the library and leaf through:
   The Ayer Directory of Publications. This lists daily, weekly, semi- and tri-weekly newspapers and consumer, business, and trade professional and special interest magazines. The listing is geographical.
   Writer's Market. This book is annually published by Writer's Digest Books, and it lists magazines published in this country. It gives you the names and addresses of the magazines and indicates what they are looking for.
   The Broadcasting Yearbook. This lists all the radio (AM and FM) and television stations in the U.S., Canada, Mexico, and the Caribbean, along with the names of the department heads. Cable systems are also included.

5. If you are willing to spend some money and you want to have a listing of all the radio and TV talk shows in the country, you might want to purchase the *Talk Show Directory.* It includes an explanation of program formats and the names of people to contact in or-

der to arrange guest interviews. Write or call: *Talk Show Directory*, 310 South Michigan Ave., Chicago IL 60604. (312)663-5580.

6. For a few dollars you can purchase the *Directory of Concert Music Stations* from Concert Music Broadcasting Penthouse, East Terminal Tower, Cleveland OH 44113.

Of course, if your concert is coordinated by a concert presenter, he will no doubt have contacts with the local media. But, the more ideas and inspiration you supply him with, the more materials you take the time to mail, and the more willing you are to do radio and TV shows, the better the prognosis for a healthy box office.

PUBLIC SERVICE ANNOUNCEMENTS

Radio and television stations are licensed every three years by the Federal Communications Commission. One of the renewal requirements is that the station devote a certain percentage of its programming to public service and submit periodic reports to the FCC proving that this is the case. Thus, there are two types of public service programming: Free commercial spots (called Public Service Announcements or PSAs) and public interest programs. If your group is nonprofit, you are eligible for this kind of publicity.

If you want to investigate the possibilities, call the stations and ask for the name of the person who handles public service. Also ask for the job title. This may be public affairs director, community relations director, or community development director. When you get that person on the phone, tell him or her that you are nonprofit and you would like to know the station's requirements for submitting public service spots. Follow these requirements exactly because a lot of people are competing for the air time. Radio stations may require a lead time of over four weeks, television stations may require six to eight weeks. Don't forget to ask if there are other public service possibilities such as interviews on community affairs programs.

PSAs are aired during commercial breaks and are ten, twenty, thirty, or sixty seconds long. A radio PSA is submitted as a typewritten script to be read by an announcer or you may submit a professionally produced tape. Television PSAs can also be sent in the form of a script, but if you have horizontal thirty-five millimeter color slides, it's a plus to send them along.

Preparing the Script of Your PSA
The heading of your PSA should include:

- Your organization's name and address. (Letterhead stationery would accomplish this.)

- The name and telephone number of the publicity contact.

- The dates you want the commercial to start and stop.

Then you have to furnish copy in ten-, twenty-, thirty-, and sixty-second versions. Keep in mind the following:

- Type out the copy—double or triple spaced.

- Spell out numbers under ten and type dates with ordinal suffixes (March 25th, April 1st).

- Include phonetic spellings for foreign words and names. The announcer who's not a musician or linguist can do astonishing things to the pronunciation of Fantasiestücke (fahn-tah-ZEE-shtuik), for example, or Boccherini (bo-ke-REE-nee).

- Use short, active words and sentences—these will have the most impact.

It will be necessary to time out your copy in a normal conversational voice (listen to radio announcers and gauge their speed). A word count will give you a *rough* idea of time:

10 seconds	10-15 words
20 seconds	25-40 words
30 seconds	55-65 words
60 seconds	120-125 words

Remember—Ticket prices may not be mentioned in a PSA. Just state the phone number to call for information. Also, you have no control over the scheduling of your PSA. They often air during off-peak hours when commercial space has not been sold, but you'd be amazed how many people manage to hear them anyway.

SOME HINTS FOR A TV OR RADIO INTERVIEW

All of your efforts have resulted in a major coup—you've been invited to be interviewed on a radio or television program.

Congratulations. But your work isn't over yet! You've got some preparation to do to be sure that the charming, vital, and multifaceted person you are comes across well over the airways.

the covington
string quartet

3120 E. 4th Place
Port Charles, Oklahoma 74104
918-776-1175

PUBLIC SERVICE ANNOUNCEMENT

For further information, contact:
Linda Reis (918)776-1175

Re: October 3, 1983 Concert
For Release: September 21, 1983
Kill Date: October 3, 1983

(ten seconds)

ENJOY THE EXQUISITE ARTISTRY OF THE COVINGTON
STRING QUARTET . . . IN CONCERT AT RANKIN HALL,
OCTOBER 3RD AT EIGHT P.M. FOR INFORMATION CALL
657-8876.

(twenty seconds)

AN EXCITING EVENT IN THE CONCERT HALL WILL BE
PROVIDED BY THE COVINGTON STRING QUARTET . . .
OCTOBER 3RD AT EIGHT P.M. AT RANKIN HALL ON CEN-
TER STREET. TICKETS AVAILABLE NOW AT THE BOX OF-
FICE, OR CALL 657-8876 FOR INFORMATION. THAT'S 657-
8876. THE COVINGTON STRING QUARTET!

(thirty seconds)

THE WASHINGTON POST DESCRIBED THE COVINGTON
STRING QUARTET AS "SPIRITED AND MUSICALLY CAP-
TIVATING." NOW, YOU CAN HEAR THEM IN CONCERT
AT RANKIN HALL ON FRIDAY EVENING OCTOBER 3RD
AT EIGHT P.M. THEIR EXCITING PROGRAM WILL FEA-
TURE THE WORLD PREMIER OF RONALD HAUGER'S
"QUARTET." TICKETS ARE ON SALE AT THE BOX OFFICE,
OR CALL 657-8876 FOR INFORMATION. THAT'S 657-8876.
HEAR ONE OF THE NATION'S FINEST YOUNG ENSEM-
BLES . . . THE COVINGTON STRING QUARTET. DON'T
MISS IT!

REMEMBER: It's better to run a bit long and let the station trim than
not to supply enough copy.

Be sure to send a cover letter on official stationery. This should be
brief and include a description of your organization. You must also certify
your nonprofit status.

1. Sit down and decide what it is you really want to get across and how you might do it clearly, warmly, and naturally. Anecdotes are the nicest, most human way to demonstrate your points, and people enjoy and remember them long after they've forgotten statistics. Once you've outlined the topics you wish to discuss, type up a list of suggested questions the interviewer could ask you. These questions should lead to answers that show you to be a talented, interesting human being. Send this list to the interviewer along with some background material such as bios, fact sheets, articles, brochures, etc.

2. If you are appearing with another member or members of your ensemble, make sure everyone has his say. Decide ahead of time who will handle this or that topic and who will relate which anecdotes.

3. Try to clear your mind of technical jargon or insiders' terms. Not everyone in the listening audience holds degrees in music and you risk someone not following you and feeling left out.

4. About dressing for television: Stay away from white shirts, pale dresses or suits, glossy fabrics, and busy patterns. Also, wear no more than a touch of red, as it doesn't reproduce well. Lots of stripes and dots can appear to strobe and bleed. Avoid large shiny jewelry or anything that might produce a glare on camera. Women should wear daytime street makeup.

5. Don't look at the TV camera or monitors. Look at the host/hostess/ interviewer and speak in a natural voice. It's all right to direct a comment or question to another guest occasionally.

6. Address the program host or hostess by first name, but don't overdo it; it doesn't sound sincere.

7. If the host or hostess seems to be searching for a question, it's all right for you to try to fill the gap and smooth things over by offering a statement or comment.

Two more things to remember: if you want a tape of the interview, ask about it before the taping and save yourself postproduction costs. Also, always send a thank-you note to the interviewer or host. He or she will appreciate the courtesy.

THE PUBLICIST

There is a lot you can do yourself to earn some media attention, but there comes a time in all good careers when the need for a professional becomes apparent. The role of the publicist in a musician's life seems to be another one of those mysteries—why do you need one? When do you need one? Why do they charge so much and what do they do that a manager doesn't? People often tend to dismiss the idea of a publicist as "too Madison Avenue," but a true professional can build an artist's career, and is a valuable resource person to know about.

First of all, a good publicist is a person with a fertile and creative mind, a sense for a good news angle, strong writing skills, and the determination to bring you to the attention of the public in the proper light. He or she has fresh eyes and can pinpoint the most newsworthy aspects of your situation. No matter how exciting your life, the events of it become integrated into the rhythm of your days; you may be sitting on "news" and not even know it! This is where a trained, objective mind can help.

A publicist will have to be enthusiastic about your talent and have the understanding of the profession to position you in the marketplace. Then, he will have to spend a great deal of time talking with you and your manager (if you have one) and reading your materials and reviews. Only then can he design a certain strategy or campaign.

This strategy has two aims—first, to excite the media personnel enough to assign you coverage or air time; and second, to present the right message to the public so that you gain people's understanding and enthusiasm. To accomplish this, a publicist has to give you a great deal of "think-time" while continuing to nurture relationships within the media world. It is then the publicist's job to create and send on a continuing flow of interesting information about you and your events to these connections. Add up the time, the energy, the skills, and the administration costs and you'll better understand the high fees.

"What Exactly Are Those Fees?"
Well, they are variable and therefore difficult to discuss, but there are generally two kinds of fee structures:

1. A per project fee. (You hire the publicist to accomplish a very specific job, such as the publicizing of one concert.)

2. A monthly retainer fee. (The publicist is hired to continually seek general publicity and publicize individual performances.)

The publicist will name a fee for a specific project. For example, a performance would no doubt need at least three months of pre-planning, so the sum would be based on that. The quotes that reached my ears were $1,000 and sometimes double that figure. A monthly retainer fee can range from $200 to over $1200 a month. The amount of time you should allow to try out this expensive undertaking requires careful consideration.

It's difficult to monitor initial results for several reasons. It takes the publicist time to introduce you to his contacts in the media world and persuade them to make room for you. Also, most magazines are laid out four to five months ahead of time and a story about you may not break for six months to a year because of this. Therefore, a nine- to twelve-month grace period or try-out is what you'll probably have to grant in order to properly assess what the publicist has accomplished.

A few publicists offer contracts, but most work with a letter of agreement. This simply spells out and confirms that you'll be working together for a specified amount of time, for a certain amount of money.

"When Do I Need a Publicist?"

When your career is moving and there's good, solid activity that could use the proper enhancement. There must be a story behind you that the publicist can work with as well as newsworthy events on the horizon such as a concert or record. Without this, a publicist would have little to say or build on. You have also got to have the maturity and seasoning to deal with the interviews and the increased activity that should come about as a result of the campaign. Most important, you must know yourself and be able to outline realistically what you want the publicist to accomplish.

"What Are the First Steps Once I Hire the Publicist?"

After getting to know you, the publicist will prepare a press kit. This is an information packet which introduces you to the media and offers them background and materials for reproduction. It almost always includes biographical matter, fact sheets and a concert/opera appearance calendar, repertoire listings, reviews and article reproductions, program bios, and lists of questions or topics with which you are comfortable (for radio/TV interviewers). At least three 8x10 photographs—different poses—will be positioned in the press kit.

The publicist will then begin to seed ideas for features (via the telephone and pitch letters), request interviews, and write many types of press releases to stimulate reviews and coverage. A lot of publicists rehearse their clients for live interviews and offer fashion advice.

As things progress, he will parlay publicity into even more publicity, and, excuse the Hollywoodese, try to keep the "heat" on you. This should increase the demand for your appearances and raise your "asking" fee.

So far, I seem to be talking about the ideal publicist and the ideal, ever-hard-working and talented client. But reality does not always match this pretty picture. Make note of a few clues.

Your publicist should be in constant contact with you, work cooperatively with your manager and be accessible. If he doesn't seem enthusiastic about your talent, doesn't report on activity or connections generated, and doesn't present you in a truthful, realistic light—brace yourself. You're in trouble. Take a good hard look at your press book and some press releases. If the writing is lackluster and the assemblage looks indifferent, make a note of it. However, some publicists are more powerful in person or on the phone, so keep this in mind also. For your part, remember that a publicist is entitled to a life too, so try to contain your phone calls within working· hours if possible and don't be a pest.

You must understand that there will be periods of less activity than others; just because you don't see a lot happening doesn't mean nothing is *developing*. Give it time. On the other hand, if your publicist does get a feature for you, don't expect one every month.

There are several unknowns present at all times in this situation: your story, your publicist, the arbitrary decisions of the media people, and plain old luck and timing.

"Do I Need a Manager and a Publicist?"

Once again, it depends. The manager works within the network of the music business. He sells you "inside" to the conductors and concert presenters. To accomplish this, he spends a great deal of time talking with these people, at conventions, on the phone, and through letters and mailings. Then, when he secures a booking for you, he negotiates the fees and contracts and handles the logistics of travel, lodging, and local transportation. He may also spend a certain amount of time generating publicity, but this is really not his major function. The manager's hard-earned reputation and relationships within the business are the connections you need for jobs. The publicist, on the other hand, has the reputation and relationships with the media which can bring your name and message to the outside world. This will increase the demand for your talents. So, to answer your question, some artists have a manager and a publicist and some do quite well with a manager, their own "nose" for news, and some hustling.

During the preparation of this chapter I spoke to a number of musicians about their feelings on the value of having a publicist. One young successful violinist expressed the ambivalence that many of them seem to feel: "I'm 75 percent in favor," he said, "but the monthly fee is still pretty hard to swallow." Then he added, "You know, most musicians complain about the artist-publicist situation. If you press the point, though, they all admit to having one or *wanting* one. Getting yourself known is the name of the game."

CHAPTER 10

Planning a Debut Recital: A Twelve-Month Count-Down

CHANCES ARE YOU'LL participate in two production extravaganzas in your lifetime. One is a wedding. The other—equally nerve-wracking—is a debut recital. They both require months of preproduction planning and a huge expenditure of money and energy. The wedding industry, however, is definitely ahead in the organization department. The bride is counseled all the way and for a few dollars she can purchase a magazine which will give her a checklist so all is ready for the big day. Taking my cue from this established system, I'm going to break down the planning stages of a recital, month by month, so that it doesn't seem so incredibly overwhelming. The point is to do a lot early, a manageable amount each month, and earmark plenty of time for practicing and ironing out the wrinkles. We are out to maximize your chances of getting that all-important review.

Before we get started, let's look at some of the budget items for which you may have to allocate money:

- Rental of hall

- Accompanist and instrumental fees

- Coaching fees

- Printing of flyers, posters, press releases, tickets, programs, and program notes

- Mailing and postage

- Concert apparel

- Recording

- Piano tuning

- Piano rental

- Recital manager

- Photographer

- Graphic designer

- Mailing lists

- Music licensing fees

- Reception

- Newspaper and radio ads

- Box office

- Ushers and stage hands

As you'll soon see, the first step is to book a hall. Get to know the concert halls in your city. Attend a concert and think about the acoustics, the piano, and the number of seats. Is the hall reviewed regularly? Then, call and ask for rate sheets and time tables. What are you getting for the fee? What extra services could you purchase? Don't compare or make decisions when you hear the basic fee. A lower fee may give you nothing but the "real estate" for the concert. You may then be forced to spend hundreds more (in an often inconvenient way) for piano rental, tuning, recording, ushers, and other hidden expenses.

Do all of this groundwork early. A popular hall may be booked more than a year in advance.

Now realistically assess your public. For whom will you be performing? This assessment will affect your budget considerably, so wipe away any grandiose fantasies. In the case of debut recitals, the relatively unknown name of the artist does not draw hordes of people. Your audience will consist of friends and relatives cheering you on and, if you've papered the house (handed out a lot of complimentary tickets), you might build a potential audience for your next concert (more about this later). So, it might be smarter to spend more money on personal invitations and a reception for your core coterie. Think this over.

The following schedule is not iron-clad; you have quite a few options and there's room for it to breathe. So! Feel free to move the months about a bit, but don't go too far afield and *don't* let it snowball on you.

12 Months Ahead

☐ Book a hall. When you get a choice of dates, check one that is not too close to a holiday. Try to find out what else is going on in the city that date—too many concerts minimize your chance of a review. (Weekends may pose a problem as there are too many performances and often too few critics on duty.) Also, keep in mind that a lot of people are music-glutted after the first week in May. Take the weather into consideration: A snowstorm would definitely rain on your parade.

☐ Prepare a budget. A well-planned debut in a large city may cost well over $5,000. Put the money into an account for this project. There will be no time to scare it up later.

☐ Decide on the program and engage other instrumentalists.

☐ Decide if you're going to hire a recital manager* and hire him/her now. The manager will schedule you from here on.

☐ Book your program as many places as possible so you can do audience-attended run-throughs within six weeks of your debut. Call colleges, your parents' friends with large homes, churches, etc. You may be able to convince some of these organizations to pay your transportation costs and even a fee.

9 Months Before

☐ Begin assembling your mailing list. Don't forget that a third class mailing must be in ZIP code order. (A computer could unscramble it. See Chapter 6.) Everyone I spoke to said this was the messiest, most troublesome part of the production, so get going! Check what lists you might want to purchase (for example, if you're an early music group, you might contact another early music group and buy their list). Also, ask the director of the concert hall if there is a house mailing list you could use. Tell the list broker to print it

---

*I have opted to use the title "recital manager" to describe the professional you hire to coordinate the production of your recital. You will no doubt hear him referred to as a "concert presenter" but because a concert presenter is also the title of a person who *hires* artists and presents them on series, I'll not confuse the subject further.

out in ZIP code order. Never leave home without a mailing list notebook—you'll always be running into someone who should be added to your list.

☐ If you decide to do a bulk rate mailing, get a permit so you have an indicia that can be printed on flyers. (See Chapter 6.) If you've hired a recital manager, you can probably use his or hers and save yourself the time at the post office plus the $80 fee.

☐ Collect and keep separate a list of all reviewers from newspapers and other publications as well as radio stations that might publicize your concert. (See Chapter 9.) Press releases and personal calls will go to these people and businesses, so get names, addresses, phone numbers, and individual deadline requests. Write these deadlines in on the calendar.

7 Months Before

☐ Have your photos taken for flyers, posters, programs, and publicity. You'll no doubt need head shots and full body shots.

☐ Start looking for a graphic designer to prepare your flyer and poster. Prepare yourself for the first meeting. (See Chapter 6.)

6 Months Before

☐ Hire a graphic designer. Schedule your first meeting.

☐ Write, or have someone write, your bio and copy so you can type it up for the first meeting with the designer.

☐ Get your recital gown/shoes/lingerie or tuxedo. Do not minimize the importance of your audience's first impression. *Get professional guidance if you need it!*

4 Months Before

☐ Your graphic designer should be hard at work on your flyer.

☐ If the hall does not provide a recording engineer, hire one.

☐ Check out the ad rates, dates, and specifications for the Sunday papers.

☐ Gather program notes and translations.

*Also, read Chapter 8 of *The Art of the Song Recital* by Shirlee Emmons and Stanley Sonntag—Schirmer Books.

☐ Arrange reception place and caterer or line up friends to handle the logistics. A restaurant could handle a crowd.

3 Months Before

☐ Flyer and poster mechanicals should be off to printer.

☐ Write, or have someone write, the press release. (See Chapter 9.)

☐ Decide what newspaper ad and radio spots are to say. Write in on this schedule when the copy and money should be sent in.

2 Months Before

☐ Print or photocopy press release.

☐ Print program.

☐ Print tickets if hall doesn't.

☐ Type and photocopy papering vouchers if you decide to paper the house. (See example, this chapter.)

☐ Print personal invitations, if desired. These will go to friends and family and personal mailing list.

☐ Sort and bundle and label bulk rate mailing. (See Chapter 6.)

6 Weeks Before

☐ Send out third class mailing.

☐ Begin concertizing the program.

☐ Send out press releases (if they are requested six weeks before. Notate on this list deadlines for other newspapers, but don't send anything before you read the section in this chapter regarding critic notification).

4 Weeks Before

☐ If you're doing a New York City debut, send press mailing to the *New York Times*.

☐ Send out first class mailing with personal notes or invitations.

☐ Send a personal note and flyer to managers and local concert presenters (the people who could hire you in the future) that you wish to come hear you. Enclose complimentary tickets.

☐ Make appointment for piano to be tuned if hall doesn't arrange.

☐ Talk someone reliable into the role of page turner.

3 Weeks Before

☐ Distribute posters to music stores and other businesses. Distribute your flyer everywhere. *Never leave the house without flyers, tape, and thumb tacks.*

2 Weeks Before

☐ Women, make an appointment to have your hair and nails done the day of the debut, and if you need a makeup artist, book now. Men, think about getting your hair trimmed within the next two weeks.

1 Week Before

☐ Confirm by phone the recording engineer, caterer, etc. If you are catering it yourself call the liquor store and order the wine or champagne to be delivered to reception area.

☐ Distribute paper vouchers.

☐ Type a "Performance Checklist" which will notate everything you need to have with you that night. Do not trust yourself to remember these details later. (See appendices.)

2 Days Before

☐ Do dress rehearsal in hall.

☐ Deliver programs to the hall.

1 Day Before

☐ Pack concert clothing and paraphernalia. Your dress/tux should be hanging out in a garment bag.

☐ Shop for the food you will eat the day of the performance and make a written list of how you'll schedule that day along.

☐ Reserve a cab to pick you up or make arrangements for transportation to hall. Remember Rhoda's wedding?

THE BIG DAY!

☐ Keep your hair appointment.

☐ Eat the food you bought at an hour right for you.

☐ Try to relax and enjoy it!

Sounds like a major undertaking, doesn't it? It is. It probably didn't take long before you thought, "Hey! When do I practice and rehearse? After all, I'm the artist, not the publicist/presenter/gofer!" Yes. Now you understand why people sometimes allot a considerable amount of money to hire professionals to take care of these details.

A recital manager *may:*

• Write the copy for your brochure and posters and act as liaison with the graphic designer, printer, and mailing house. He or she will probably let you use the bulk rate indicia and save you money and time at the post office.

• Write and mail the press release and try to attract critical attention.

• Obtain other mailing lists and work toward audience development. Paper the house intelligently.

• Act as wardrobe consultant.

• Act as liaison with the concert hall and make sure everything is running smoothly.

• Place ads in the papers and magazines (subject to your budget) and write and book radio spots.

• Hold your hand and help you through.

Here's the bad news. These professionals are expensive and they are so busy performing similar services for other people that you don't always get "tuned-in" attention. They often do their job and just that. They also cannot guarantee you a review.

You must know yourself. If you can't deal with details, deadlines, the writing of copy and general administrative tasks, hire (and pay for) a recital manager to do these jobs. If you live a distance away from the city in which you are making a debut, it is perhaps wisest to hire a recital manager. You find a recital manager by asking for recommendations from friends or colleagues, or from the director of the recital hall. You can also look at the write-ups of managers in the yearly *Musical America Directory* and isolate which managers handle concert presentation. These write-ups also list the names of artists presented in that year and you could give two or three a call and find out how happy they were with the services.

Was the manager accessible, professional, and on schedule? Were his resources and relationships with the graphic designer, printer, hall personnel, etc., top-notch? Could he write good press releases and biographical material for flyers and could he stimulate audience development? Was he sympathetic and reassuring? If two or three artists answer these questions affirmatively, you can most likely proceed with confidence.

If, on the other hand, your uncle is a printer, your best friend is a graphic designer, your other best friend wants to throw a lavish reception at her recently remodeled townhouse apartment and your spouse has a flair for writing—*plus you have strong (and I mean very strong) organizational skills)*—you can present a debut yourself and just possibly do it more effectively, in your style, and save a few thousand dollars. But keep in mind your stamina and labor and the millions of other things you have to do each day to keep self and soul together. Also, I find that when people do me favors, I hesitate to push them about deadlines and this could be deadly for your debut and, subsequently, for your friendship. Better to be businesslike, I think.

CRITICAL CRITIC NOTIFICATION INFORMATION

One of the primary reasons for giving a debut is to receive critical attention. The following information should give you your best shot:

1. Call the Music Editor of the paper and inquire about their working procedures—when do they need your press release mailing? Would they tolerate more than one notification or a follow-up phone call? The *New York Times* needs your *one* mailing four weeks in advance of your recital. It should be addressed only to "Music Editor." This is the one time that a specific name will *not* work in your favor.

2. Prepare a mailing of the following items:
   - The press release.
   - An 8x10 black-and-white photo (fully captioned as per the discussion in Chapter 9). The photos are handled at a different desk by the photo editor and must be able to travel without the rest of your packet.
   - A recital flyer which lists your biographical information and the total program.
   - A set of tickets. Ask the manager of the box office to help you assign the critics' seats—he or she will know who likes to sit where.

3. Do not neglect to mention that this is your *debut*. The editor will need to know this.
4. Do not ask for the return of your picture.
5. If some part of the mailing outlined in #2 is not available by the deadline, send everything you can, with all the pertinent facts and a cover letter explaining that you'll send the missing items as soon as you grab them off the press.

PAPERING THE HOUSE

You've probably been wondering why I'm making such a point of papering the house. On first hearing it seems an unhappy phrase. It somehow implies that you are not an SRO performer. My answer to that is, *why should you be?* This is your debut—it is by definition a hint of what is to come, a first introduction. Papering accomplishes a lot of things for you. First, it's a psychological boost. (If you've ever walked out on a stage and performed to a lot of empty seats, you'll know what I mean.) Seeing a lot of people may just give you the "up" frame of mind you need to really distinguish yourself. And, if you do, those breathing human beings will go out and spread the word about you (become your ambassadors, so to speak) and no doubt line up early at the box office *with cash* for your next event.

There are, however, intelligent and not-so-intelligent ways to handle the papering process. The wrong route is to pull two hundred tickets from the box office and distribute them randomly. Most of them will not be used and your box office person may never recover from the shortage of good tickets the night of the concert. A better way would be to type up and photocopy a two-sided voucher that can be exchanged for a ticket. It should look like the illustration on the next page.

Instruct your box office people to hand over a complimentary ticket after the person fills out their name and address. You then have additions to your mailing list!

You can staple bunches of these vouchers and distribute them at schools and colleges, senior citizen centers, hospitals, etc. Call first and send them to the right person in the right section of the organization.

AFTERNOTE

So! You've done yourself proud, drunk a bottle of champagne and you're going to bed for a week, luxuriating in the fact that you've no more details and deadlines. Maybe you're even considering a little trip to the Bahamas

FRONT

DEBUT RECITAL!
TAFELMUSIK

Exchange this voucher at the box office for
one complimentary ticket.

On: Tuesday, February 14, 1984
At: 8:00 p.m.
Merkin Concert Hall, 129 W. 67 Street,
New York City

BACK

Name: _____

Address: _____

_____

_____

for the R&R you certainly deserve. *Cancel that trip and get out of bed!* There is crucial work to be done. You are now into the follow-up phase of this production and it might be the most important one in terms of your performing future.

1. Get to the box office and collect your voucher slips before they get lost. Update your mailing list.

2. If (I'm keeping my fingers crossed) you got a favorable review, this is the time to contact that management firm you've been trying to woo. Get to them while it's "news." Old news is *no* news! Also, write to as many people who book concerts as possible. You might just line up some jobs from this new contact supported by an exciting review.

A PHILOSOPHY

The saddest thing about this whole process is that there's no way to be guaranteed a review, good or bad or tepid. You have to undertake this project understanding this. All the public relations, publicity, novenas, and good intentions may just not do the trick.

So why would you do it? Seems a bit masochistic (not to mention expensive) when you think about it. You would of course want a rave review, but, if that doesn't come to pass, think about this. You are still getting the publicity and exposure. It can be a showcase for agents or presenters to hear you and if you wish to build a teaching studio, it's a nice way to attract students.

A debut recital is a personal stretch for you, a memorable occasion for your family and friends, and a potential way to build yourself a following. All of these benefits should help make the expenditure of time, money, and nervous energy worthwhile. Hold on to the things of value.

CHAPTER 11

Networking and Other Acts of Courage

TALENT, TECHNIQUE, and lucky breaks are the underpinnings of successful careers—or so I thought throughout my years at music school. However, the more I began to examine the careers of colleagues and friends, the more I was able to trace the provenance of engagements and opportunities to networking systems: friends, teachers, professional acquaintances—people who cared and thought enough of a person to make recommendations and offer help. Networking is an essential element of professional life.

It's true that no man is an island. We need each other for so many things—companionship, support, *and* information. One person sees and hears only so much. A network, though, multiplies senses and covers a great deal of territory. Thus, someone may be able to supply you with the name of a graphic designer; you may be able to offer a friend information about an audition date. Be a colleague, not a competitor. You'll not only go further, you'll have a better, more comfortable time of things. Auditions, master classes, rehearsals, performances, and parties all bring you into contact with people and are excellent opportunities for networking.

As you read these stories, you'll realize that there's another qualification required for the job description Professional Musician. It's courage. The courage to reach out to people, to risk asking for something you need or want. The person who appropriately networks or takes a chance is not a user or a grandiose personality. He's a person who knows how to give, knows what he has to offer and to whom, and who has the guts to see that things happen. The following active professionals have talent, technique, and determination. They also understand the need for networking and other acts of courage.

Sylvia Kahan, pianist:

This saga begins in the Cleveland airport and ends several years later on a luxury cruise ship traveling through the Norwegian fjords. But first I have to take you back to my graduate school days at Michigan State University.

Each term, the Juilliard Quartet would come and give concerts and student ensemble coaching. I was particularly frustrated because my piano trio could have benefited from their expertise, but the Quartet's schedule was always full. It so happened that two weeks before the Quartet was scheduled to arrive, I was flying home to New York and had a brief layover in Cleveland. I was in an airport phone booth speaking to a friend when, who should appear before the window but Joel Krosnick, the cellist of the Juilliard Quartet. I had never met him before, but I yanked open the door and said, "Wait a minute, I have to talk to you!" He stopped and looked bewildered. I rapidly explained that I had long admired the Juilliard Quartet and wanted to have a coaching at Michigan State, but was having difficulty making the arrangements. Joel very kindly agreed to find the time to coach my trio. And this was the first in a four-year network of events.

I subsequently moved to New York City and, two years into my stay, ran into Joel Krosnick in the subway. We caught up a bit on the intervening years and exchanged phone numbers. Two weeks later, Joel called and told me he was planning two weeks of master classes in New York City and asked if I'd like to accompany. Would I! I was delighted and it was a marvelous experience. One of the participants was a fine cellist named Barbara Bogatin. The following year I received a call from her. She was in a real predicament: she was supposed to perform a recital in ten days and her accompanist had suddenly become seriously ill. Could I learn the music quickly and perform the concert with her on such short notice? Oddly enough, I had just played two of the pieces for a cellist in the Naumburg competiton. I hastily learned the rest of the program and Barbara and I started rehearsing immediately. It was a fortunate collaboration and the concert was a success.

Two months later, Barbara called me and asked if I would be interested in joining a chamber music ensemble to perform on a cruise ship for the entire summer. Salary, plus all expenses paid, plus full participation in the cruise program to Europe, England, and Scandinavia!

Well, it happened. I did it. I played Grieg at the Arctic Circle with the midnight sun in the background. So, I guess the moral of this story is, *never* close your eyes in a phone booth!

Jean R. Dane, violist,
Composers String Quartet

Amazing how interconnected the music world is. Its "grapevine" is marvelously useful and effective—and also, occasionally, crosses one's present with one's distant past. Once, several years ago, after a call from a former viola student looking for a quartet opening, I called up an old friend, a cellist I hadn't seen or heard from in about twelve years. I had heard he was in a quartet, and then had heard recently that they were looking for a violist: were they still? They had just found one, it turned out, but it was fun to be in touch anyway, after all those years. Then just a few weeks later an old friend called me—this was a violinist I hadn't seen or heard from in at least ten years, so there was a lot of catching up to do there too. He said he'd known I was in the Composers String Quartet, but wondered if I might be able to get away to do a special chamber music series with his group. I couldn't, but I put him in touch with that former student, she took the job, and it worked out beautifully for all of them. Though not the permanent position she was looking for, it was a challenging and satisfying experience, gave her some excellent exposure, and added to her credentials and her "points of contact" along the grapevine. As I say, it can be a very effective one—the one requirement being that we all keep feeding it information. Several of my old students do call or write, three or four times a year, just to say hello, tell me what and where and with whom they're playing, pass along odd bits of gossip, or ask advice on anything from

"Should I take this job?" to "Should I marry this tympanist?" to "What bowing do you use in this phrase?"

James Tyeska, bass-baritone:

A few years ago I was invited to sing a concert performance of *Porgy and Bess* with the Fort Worth Symphony. The morning of the performance, I read in the newspaper that the orchestra would open its next season with Beethoven's "Ninth Symphony," soloists to be announced. The Ninth! I had always found it inspiring, always wanted to sing it, and now here was the opportunity!

The *Porgy* performance went very well and as the audience rose to their feet, the soloists and Maestro John Giordano bowed and withdrew to the wings. Standing backstage, I said, "Maestro, I noticed you're doing the Ninth Symphony next season, soloists to be announced." I smiled and continued, "I'd like to be considered for the part." He replied, "You want it, you've got it!"

This incident was a great lesson. Now, when I work with an orchestra or an opera company, I make it my business to talk with the person in charge. I get feedback about my work and I ask if they might have something for me in the future. Believe me, it works. Don't wait for your agent or manager to do it for you. This is your moment!

Johnathan Feldman, pianist:

In the spring of 1980, I returned from a tour with an artist managed by Shaw Concerts. Several details needed to be worked out and I decided to see Mr. Shaw directly. While there, we got to talking about the "music business" and I decided to take the bull by the horns and discuss my career directions with him. It's not every day that one gets the opportunity to speak with the head of such a prestigious agency. Not only was I surprised with my own boldness for having taking the initiative, I was thrilled to be getting such advice form this generous man who was taking so much time from his busy schedule. I was in Mr. Shaw's office for almost an hour and left with my head filled with ideas.

The following fall, I received a call from the Shaw office asking me if I would be interested in meeting and playing with

Nathan Milstein (who had been with Mr. Shaw for many years). Apparently there were some schedule problems with Mr. Milstein's usual accompanist and he was looking for some-one to play the American dates. I was told to go to his hotel the next day (Wednesday) prepared to play the C minor Beethoven sonata, a piece I had not played before. I hung up the phone and got the music out and I practiced . . . all day . . . night, and the following morning. Of course you can't real-ly learn a work like that in a day, but I put as many of those notes into my fingers as was possible, and took a deep breath as I made my way over to the East Side.

We played for an hour when Mr. Milstein told me that he had someone else to audition on Friday and would I return on Saturday. That gave me three more days to practice and ob-sess. Saturday came and I went back to play. After a while, Mr. Milstein asked me if I would like to play the tour with him. I re-member being so excited that there were a few seconds of si-lence while I swallowed a couple of times and finally uttered something like "Yes."

This all came about because Harold Shaw was familiar with my abilities and knew (from our talk) of my desire to work.

Jane Taylor, bassoonist,
The Dorian Wind Quintet:

It's a lucky thing I was busy freelancing in 1961 when the Dorian Wind Quintet was formed because each step we took cost so much money, all coming from our pockets. Our debut in October of that year was a great success and earned us some fine reviews. By 1962 we had performed some modest concerts and had enough reviews for a flyer, but we really needed a Eu-ropean tour because the European reviews would carry seri-ous weight. Unlike today, it was not routine for chamber groups to travel abroad. The problem was that nobody knew us over there, our few reviews would not be enough to sell the Quintet and we couldn't afford to buy ourselves a concert tour—a standard practice of many American soloists.

We embarked upon an expensive gamble: to tape the Quintet and make a record. Our flutist at that time was John Perras, who was very talented in electronics and had a great deal of experience. We rented the basement of the Turtle Bay Music School and some professional tape equipment and with John's brother pressing the "on" and "off" buttons we recorded a good variety of pieces for two sides of a record. In our spare time we did our own editing and then had the records professionally pressed. Next, we sent them out to every radio station and manager in Europe for whom we could find an address. It was a "shotgun" approach (aim at everything, you might hit something) and it did net us a short tour from which we got good and useful reviews. Although we hadn't planned it, there were some records left over which, sent around the U.S., turned up some American dates.

We've returned to Europe twelve times. Some concerts were a direct result of that record mailing. Other dates came from contacts made while abroad, and still others came from personal contacts of newer Dorian members. We also got help, from time to time, from the U.S. State Department.

At the time we were putting our hard-earned money into this and other projects, we told ourselves that it was an investment in the Dorian's future but I think we only half believed it. Looking back from a perspective of twenty years, it is clear that that investment was actually a bargain.

Eugene Drucker, violinist,
The Emerson Quartet

Networking has undoubtedly advanced our career in the Emerson Quartet. I feel that an ensemble is at an advantage in this arena because each member's career connections are extended and multiplied by the connections of the other members. There's a kind of geometrical progression of contacts resulting in a career momentum that most individuals could not generate alone.

For instance, I used to be a violinist with the New York Chamber Soloists. Melvin Kaplan, the director and manager of the group, learned that I had a string quartet and expressed an interest in managing us. We signed with him in late 1976. Looking back now, I see that we just might not have survived the embryonic stage of our career if it had taken too long to find an agent and if we'd had no concert schedule to look forward to. We needed the impetus and advance in our professional life at that particular time.

The other violinist in our ensemble, Philip Setzer, grew up in Cleveland. Both his parents are violinists in the Cleveland Orchestra and Phil studied with Rafael Druian, then concertmaster of the orchestra. In the fall of 1979, Rafael was the head of the string department at the Hartt School of Music and he invited us to audition for the position of Quartet-in-Residence. It was a succesful audition, and a year later we began the residency with a concert in which Scott Nickrenz (then a violist on the faculty) played a Brahms quintet with us. Scott is the director of the chamber music section of the Spoleto Festival and he invited us to perform in Charleston and Italy the next season.

Our connection with Spoleto introduced us to Charles Wadsworth who announced the program at the Charleston concerts. He asked us to become members of the Chamber Music Society of Lincoln Center! This was possibly the most important single thing that happened in our career.

So, the sequence was Setzer-Druian-Hartt-Nickrenz-Spoleto-Wadsworth-Lincoln Center. Luck and timing (we were in the right places at the right times) were not inessential to this chain of events. But if we had not worked very hard, supported each other, and played our best at some of those crucial times, the sequence would not have progressed as rapidly and produced such gratifying results for us all.

Karen Beardsley, soprano:

It was the summer of 1982 and Joel Bloch from Columbia Artists Management had been invited upstate New York to give a master class for the Lake George apprentices—which included me. This was an important summer because my career seemed to be taking off and I felt strongly that I wanted and needed management . . . and I immediately set my sights on Columbia!

Joel Bloch's master class lasted over an hour and I hung on every word he said and took notes voraciously. At the close, he gave us his phone number and invited us to call him for professional advice on our résumés, pictures, audition repertoire, etc. I couldn't believe it. To me, this seemed like the opportunity of a lifetime—professional counseling from one of the top managers in the world . . . I couldn't wait to call him!

But actually *doing* that was a different story. I remember

that morning clearly. There were my notes and his number in front of me, my hand on the phone . . . why was it so hard to dial that number? I was scared to death, scared to death and driven to do it at the same time. I sat there until my husband, Maitland, came into the kitchen and said, "Do it!" I said, "I can't" and he just looked at me and said, "Dial!" The next thing I heard was Joel Bloch's voice on the other end saying, "Yes, come see me . . . in fact, come right now." I hung up the phone in a panic. My God, there I sat in my robe and slippers and I was supposed to be there "right now."

I showered, threw on my makeup and a fuchsia pink dress, grabbed my résumé packet and was off to 57th Street. In my mind, I wanted management and not *just* management but Columbia. What better time was there than this to present myself?

I had taken great pains to make my press kit look as professional as possible. Minutes after presenting it to Mr. Bloch, it became apparent to him that I had not come to ask advice on how to improve my résumé, but that I was actually presenting myself for his 1983 roster of artists. He read through my material quite thoroughly and then sighed deeply and said, "Miss Beardsley, your materials are very impressive, but my roster is quite full at this time. Possibly I could suggest some smaller agencies that you could call."

My heart stopped. I felt numb and pale. I will *never* forget that moment. For me, it was the moment of truth. So many thoughts flashed through my mind, but I basically had two choices. One was to say, "Thank you for your time—goodbye," the other was to take the risk and *go for it!* I decided in that split second that since I was the only one in that room, the only one who could sell me, was *me*. So I said, "Mr. Bloch, I want to be a Columbia Artist. I have the capabilities and I'm a marketable soubrette—what do I need to be worthy of your roster?" (Whew!)

Later, he told me he liked my determination and drive. But at that moment, he proceeded to coolly give me the names of the smaller agencies and helped me rewrite the opening sentence of my bio. He had been helpful, but I was terribly disappointed. I prepared to leave, thanked him for his time and as I turned to walk out the door, he stopped me and asked if I knew the aria "Glitter and Be Gay." I didn't, but I immediately said, "I can learn it!" Then he looked me straight in the eyes and said, "You learn it and come back here at two o'clock tomorrow and sing it for me in Cami Hall."

As I left the office, I glanced at my watch . . . it was 4:30 p.m. I tore home, called Richard, my coach and pianist, and told him to get over there as fast as he could. I stayed up all night memorizing (who could sleep?), and when I sang it at two the next day, Mr. Bloch seemed enormously pleased. I had previously been engaged to make my debut at the Taipei International Arts Festival in Taiwan. Mr. Bloch said, "You go to Taiwan and when you get back, call me. I want to hear your repertoire."

A month later, I called, sang my repertoire for him on the stage of Cami Hall and he said, "Come down here. I want to sign you as a Columbia Artist."

Cho Liang Lin, violinist:

Every performer owes a great debt to at least one teacher. In the case of this Taiwan-born American, it is a trinity: another performer, Israeli-born American, Itzhak Perlman, and two teachers, Hungarian-born Australian, Robert Pikler, and Kansas-born Dorothy DeLay from Medicine Lodge.

Switching from the spiritual to the scientific, these three are the links in a chain reaction that began for me in Australia in 1973 and have affected everything in my life since.

I was thirteen and had been in Australia less than a year. Everything was new to me. A new language, a new school, a new environment, new friends, and a wholly new experience—cultural shock. It was both fascinating and frightening. But dominating it all was my hunger for more guidance in playing the violin. I was not then fully aware of how fortunate I had been to be assigned to Robert Pikler. He had been ill much of that year and had been able to give me only one lesson. I was literally hungry for someone to help me with my violin.

In that state of mind, my eye caught a newspaper notice that someone named Itzhak Perlman was about to make his debut Australian tour. I had no idea who he was. Only the names of Heifetz, Oistrakh, and Stern were familiar to me. But I was curious, and got a ticket to the concert. He started with the Beethoven "Spring" Sonata. From that first note—that beautiful A—I was spellbound; not only by his beautiful sound, but by the total control he had over his instrument. It was at that moment I realized music was a huge universe I simply had to explore and that I had to find the training that would guide me into it.

Three days later, Perlman came to the Sydney Conservatorium to give a master class. I was determined to play for him, but the list of students signed up for his class was a long one. Somehow I managed to get on the list and to play the Mendelssohn Concerto for him. Because of Mr. Pikler's illness, I had not had a lesson for several months, and I did not play well. But Mr. Perlman was kind and encouraging. Maybe because he preferred not to comment on my playing, he told fascinating stories about his student days at Juilliard and a teacher named Dorothy DeLay. In particular, there were amusing anecdotes about the different approaches to teaching by this Miss DeLay and a Mr. Galamian. I knew nothing of either of them, but I came away from that session determined that somehow, somewhere, I was going to study with Dorothy DeLay.

I told Mr. Pikler about the experience. Far from being upset, as many teachers might be, he encouraged me. It was from him I learned that studying with Miss DeLay involved getting admitted to the Juilliard School. Thanks to his encouragement, and the help of friends both here and in Australia, I arrived at Juilliard in September 1975 for an audition. After my acceptance, Dean Gideon Waldrop asked me if I had a particular teacher in mind.

"Oh yes," I replied, "my teacher in Australia told me that if I could express a wish I should ask for Miss DeLay." I added, as persuasively as I knew how, "I would like very much for her to be my teacher."

He smiled and told me that Miss DeLay had already mentioned she had been impressed with my audition and he was sure she would be willing to take me. That was one of my happiest days. The wheel of good fortune was still turning for me.

In the summer of 1976, at Aspen, who should come at Miss DeLay's invitiation to give a master class? None other than Itzhak Perlman! It was my second chance to play the Mendelssohn for him. I was so excited I don't remember much about the class except that once again he was very nice and encouraging. Also, I was sure I had played better than I had the first time.

Recently when I was recording the Mendelssohn with the Philharmonica Orchestra in London for CBS Masterworks, all this came rushing back to my mind. It made me realize that all of the wonderful things that have happened to me, and the fulfilling career I now have, would not have happened if I had not heard Perlman play, and then heard him talk about Dorothy DeLay.

CHAPTER 12

Play It Again, Uncle Sam: Taxes and the Performing Artist

I HAVE TO ADMIT IT. I took a deep breath before I approached the subject of taxes. Three years ago, I barely knew what a deduction was. However, I found that once I got familiar with the phrasing and rules and organized a system, the subject wasn't all that forbidding.

Reading this chapter will not enable you to actually do your taxes yourself. Rather, its purpose is to make you aware of your everyday responsibilities so you can easily and certifiably present your total income picture to a qualified tax consultant at the end of the fiscal year. This professional can then prepare your return, saving you every bit of money you legally deserve.

I've been telling you all along that you must invest money in your career. So let's immediately discuss how you should keep records of these expenditures and why.

KEEPING TRACK OF YOUR EXPENSES

You are an artist and you earn money either by performing your craft or teaching. Sometimes, you supplement your professional income by working a job totally unrelated to music. The money you earn is subject to taxation. However, the IRS allows you to add up some of the money you *spend* in order to perfect or sustain your professional skills (and live as a private citizen) and subtract these "deductions" before arriving at the "taxable income figure" on which your taxes are calculated. In order to legally take these deductions, or even know what they total, you must keep exact and detailed records. These records will also support your claim to professional status (more about that later).

There are several ways to clarify how much you spend and to back up your deductions should the IRS choose to question you in an audit:

1. Keep a daily diary or journal of your expenses and earnings. Jot these things down in an appointment book you always carry with you *as they come about*—in the cab going to an audition, after you get off the pay phone, before you leave the photocopy store. The IRS is impressed with this kind of notation.

FEBRUARY
S M T W T F S
1 2 3 4
5 6 7 8 9 10 11
12 13 14 15 16 17 18
19 20 21 22 23 24 25
26 27 28 29

Monday 13/Feb

75¢ bus to / 75¢ from 10:00 - coaching

2.50 cab / .75 bus 1:00 - rehearsal (bring Mozart)

3.31 cab → 3:00 - meeting with agent - my house
.40 - calls into answering machine
8:00 dinner / Jim

Tuesday 14/Feb
ST. VALENTINE'S DAY

9 / ↓12 Practice !

4.86 · Photocopy Center - Mozart + Schubert
.75 / .75 2:00 · run-through for concert
4.51
mailing envelopes 6:00 - meet Jim for dinner
.20 calls into machine

Wednesday 15/Feb
$7.00 Pick up Concert dress at Cleaner's, call Jim
.75 bus / .75 9:00 - Breakfast meeting/Cathy Lewis (presenter)

$5.00 cab 1:00 Leave for Baltimore Concert
$55 round trip ticket

2. Save all checks and receipts. A canceled check made out to an individual may not hold up as proof. Fill out the memo section of the check as explicitly as possible. Get a receipt with the date, amount and nature of the expense and the signature of the person who accepted payment. You should have a receipt and, if possible, a journal entry for all expenses over $25.00. The check is further proof.

THE BASKET-ON-THE-PIANO METHOD

Okay. So you've been obsessively passionate about collecting receipts, making journal entries, etc. all year long. But comes February or March and you are dealing with hundreds of tiny receipt papers, canceled checks, and chicken scratches in your journal. Your memory refuses to be jogged. You dread adding all this up. What should you do?

Well, I've found a method whereby I throw all my receipts into a basket on my piano and every two weeks or so I haul the basket over to my typewriter and update my "financials." These are simply 8½x11 sheets of paper that I've headed with different categories of business expenses incurred. (See the list of deductions later in this chapter.) For example, one sheet categorizes *Administrative Expenses* such as stationery, postage, business entertaining etc. Other topics are listed as *Courses, Costumes and Dry Cleaning,* and *Music—Photocopying—Lp's.*

A sample would look like this:

ADMINISTRATIVE EXPENSES

2.65—3/25/83	Typewriter cartridge, Jay's Stationery
40.00—3/28/83	Postage (U.N. Concert mailing)
5.00—4/1/83	Refreshments—meeting with agent Robert Spenser
49.50—4/15/83	Long distance business phone calls
54.00—4/17/83	Business cards (Varied Printing, count 500)

I look through my diary and check book notations also. After I type up any new expenses, I put the receipts, credit card records, and canceled checks in an envelope marked with the year and topic (1983—Administrative Expenses). Before visiting my tax consultant, I simply photocopy my financial sheets and hand them over at our meeting. Because I've done a small amount of record keeping every month, it may take me two hours to gather the picture together, not two to five days of misery. (What if you had a busy concert season next February, March, and April? Where would you spare five days?) Should I be audited, the receipts, canceled checks, and credit card records are bundled together under appropriate categories and, of course, my journal entries correspondingly strengthen my assertions.

Don't drag a shopping bag full of receipts over to an accountant and plead with him to set it all straight. He will, but that leaves no time for him to view your overall situation and advise you. Plus, you'll pay more for your returns.

Monies you receive must also be recorded. An easy way is to deposit the checks into a single bank account and notate it in your checkbook or savings pass book. It's a good idea to have a separate business account. List who gave it to you and what you did to earn it. It's also advisable to keep a ledger of money earned—cash or checks. You can notate more specifically here.

You should keep your diaries and records for at least three years as the IRS has that amount of time in which to assess additional taxes. If a taxpayer omits gross income of over 25 percent of the gross income reported on the return there's a six-year statute. This means that in 1986 taxes can be assessed as far back as 1980. If you fail to file or tax fraud is suspected, the IRS can search back indefinitely. Musicians who need to prove professional status or who wish to income average (both subjects soon to be discussed) should hold on to all records for a significant time span. Your accountant can specify this length of time.

YOU AND YOUR IRS CLASSIFICATION(S)

A performing artist usually fits into three separate tax categories and will fill out different forms when accounting for various types of income and expenses.

1. A SELF-EMPLOYED PROFESSIONAL. As an artist, you intend to make a profit as a result of practicing or teaching your art. Taxes are not usually withheld from this income and the self-employed professional has to determine how much they might be.

2. AN EMPLOYEE. You collect a regular or occasional paycheck from an employer. Federal, state, and city taxes as well as FICA or Social Security are withheld by the employer.

3. A PRIVATE CITIZEN. We all qualify for this category and we have income and expenditures which are not related to business in any

way, e.g. medical expenses, stock dividends, alimony, etc. When you itemize these non-business-related deductions, it doesn't matter if you work as an employee or as a freelancer.

If you are working professionally as a musician, but must also work full time (for now) on a Wang machine to support the career foundations, and you receive interest on a savings account, you fit into all three categories just listed. These separate incomes will be accounted for on different IRS forms, so it's important to get familiar with them now, as we'll be referring to them over and over again.

If you are employed, you will need these forms and schedules:

FORM

1040	Wages, tips, and other employee compensation such as moving expenses or free lodging.
2106	Unreimbursed employee expenses.
Schedule A	Itemized deductions—should it be worth your while to itemize.

If you are a self-employed professional, these schedules may be required in addition to Form 1040.

Schedule C	Business profits and expenses.
Schedule E	Passive royalty and residual income.
Schedule SE	Computation of self-employment tax. Replaces employee withholding for social security.
Schedule A	Mentioned above.

As a private citizen you might also need Schedule A, mentioned above, and Schedule B which shows unearned income in excess of $400.00 (interest or dividends from stocks, bonds, savings accounts).

Schedule C is the big one for the self-employed performing artist. It is here that you report income received from the exercise of your art and teaching. But it is also on this form that you get "off the top" deductions. Their total is deducted from your Schedule C income on Schedule C and the result is carried over to Form 1040 which asks for your adjusted gross income. IRS Publication 334, "Tax Guide for Small Business," can tell you more about Schedule C.

Note: If you are an employed musician such as a symphony instrumentalist or a Met chorister, you report business deductions such as union dues, periodicals, uniform, and uniform maintenance etc. on Schedule A and travel/transportation expenses on Form 2106. If you work a job like this *and* teach and concertize, you would report on A, C, and 2106, depending how you incurred the expenses.

PROVING THAT YOU ARE PROFESSIONAL

People often ask, *"How can I prove that I'm a self-employed professional when I don't generate a great deal of income from my career but basically support myself with my job at the bank?"*

Understandably, the IRS has a right to question the picture here. Are you "in business" or is your music a hobby? The definitive test is whether you have an "intent" to make a profit from your self-employment. It is not necessary to make a profit. In fact, some years your expenses will far outweigh any profit.

Reviews, professional correspondence, financial records, records of union dues paid and contracts would help prove your professional standing. The harbor of safety would be if you could prove you made a profit two years out of five. This would show you are "intending" to make a profit. However, the courts are more lenient and they realize there is a very long gestation period for an artist. If you are leaving your job twice a week to go to lessons, you audition all the time, spend a lot of money taking courses and coaching and going to workshops and reading professional journals etc., this is not merely a hobby. *Diary entries are particularly supportive here.* Keep on working and deducting expenses!

If there is a question of your professional status, but you plan on making a profit within the next five years, you can delay this assessment by filling out Forms 5213 and 5214 within three years of the due date for the return of the year in which you began your business.

ARRIVING RIGHT ON SCHEDULE C: BUSINESS EXPENSES

The Schedule C deductions represent the "ordinary and necessary" expenses incurred in producing your professional income. The following partial list will clue you into these deductions. I'll go into more detail later, but look them over carefully and set your awareness so you know which

receipts and records to keep. Remember! We are talking about professional, *not* private, expenses here.

Accompanist fees
Accounting fees
Agent or management fees or retainers
Auto
Auto rental
Books (pertaining to your field)
Cabs
Coachings
Costumes: The law says that if it can be worn in the streets it's not a cos-
      tume and therefore, not deductible. A dress or suit you buy for an
      audition is *not* deductible.
Dance Clothing
Depreciation of equipment (musical instruments, typewriter, calculator,
      tape recorder, computer, photocopy machine, etc.)
Drama Coaching
Dues (professional unions or organizations)
Equipment: reeds, strings, key pads, etc.
Entertainment
Insurance premiums
Maintenance of costume clothing (laundry and dry cleaning)
Makeup for stage
Moving expenses for business purposes (check with your accountant)
Music scores
Periodicals, newspapers in your professional area (the fraction of the Arts
      & Leisure section of the *New York Times* is deductible)—trade pa-
      pers, i.e., *Back Stage, Show Business*
Piano Tuning
Parking and garage
Photography for publicity
Photostats
Postage
Printing
Professional gifts (up to $25.00 per person, per year)
Professional research
Publicity
Records—phonographic
Rehearsal fees
Rental of office or rehearsal space

Sanitation and maintenance of office
Stationery
Subscriptions (*Opera News, Keynote, High Fidelity,* etc.)
Supplies—office
Tapes
Telephone answering service
Telephone—business
Tickets to concerts or opera or theater (as they relate to your field) also,
    tickets you purchase to give to critics, managers, and concert pre-
    senters
Travel and Tolls
Utilities (for office)

The lessons, coachings, and classes you take are necessary for the maintenance or improvement of your skills for your present position and are deductible. They can easily add up to a few thousand dollars, and this kind of a deduction might be unfamiliar to a tax examiner. The examiner may try to deny the deduction and rule them "educational expenses" which are not deductible. Be prepared to fight to the finish on this one because you deserve the deduction. You can consult IRS Publication 508, "Tax Information on Educational Expenses," for ammunition for your argument. But, help clarify and detail the situation to a possible examiner by attaching a supporting schedule of your own.

Label a standard sheet of paper, "LESSONS AND COACHINGS— NECESSARY TO MAINTAIN AND IMPROVE SKILLS IN PROFESSION."

TEACHER	ADDRESS	INSTRUMENT/VOICE LESSONS
		$ _____
TEACHER	ADDRESS	COACHING
		$ _____
TEACHER	ADDRESS	DRAMA LESSONS
		$ _____

Note: It's best to do the same thing with management fees.

YOUR HOME OFFICE

The question of the home office seems to be a major preoccupation with many musicians. It's been further complicated by the recent case of the three Metropolitan Opera Orchestra members winning their case in the Second Circuit Court. I'd like to review the overall situation but remember that we are dealing here with two categories of musicians—the *self-employed* professional and the *employed* professional.

If, as a self-employed professional, you use a room in your house *exclusively* and on a *regular basis* as your principal place of business, you may deduct a proportion of your rent and utilities. If your office is in a corner of the dining room, and your rehearsal studio doubles as a place to sleep, watch television, or play Scrabble, you may not deduct. Keep in mind also that the gross income generated from your business conducted at home must be greater than certain specified deductions allocable to the use of your home as an office or studio. (Read IRS Publication #587 and speak to your accountant.)

If you are an employee, the use of the home office must also be for the *convenience of the employer* and not just appropriate and helpful in your job. (Lock this into memory; it will help you understand the next part of this drama.)

On August 19th of 1983, the U.S. Court of Appeals for the Second Circuit in New York ruled that three Metropolitan Opera Orchestra members were entitled to deduct part of their rent, electricity, and maintenance expenses allocable to the areas of their apartments where they practiced their instruments. The Commissioner of Internal Revenue had previously disallowed these deductions and assigned payment deficiencies. Collectively, the musicians petitioned the Tax Court but the IRS decision was upheld.

Undaunted, the three went to the Court of Appeals and the Judge there reversed the decision based on the section of the Internal Revenue Code that allows deduction of expenses for "a portion of the dwelling unit which is exclusively used on a regular basis" as the "principal place of business for any trade or business of the taxpayer." The deduction is available to an employee "only if the exclusive use . . . is for the convenience of the employer."

Because the Met musicians were *employees* who needed to practice at least thirty hours a week in their homes in order to maintain their standards for the Met position (the Met provided no space for this), they met, in the Court's opinion, the requirements of the provision. (The court also added that being a musician is "a strange way to make a living.")

Here comes the big *but*: This case is not over yet because the IRS may consider another appeal; there has been no announcement as yet that the Commissioner will acquiesce. At this point, nothing has changed, and you must remember that this ruling, to date, applies *only to this specific case*, not to the greater body of musicians. If you wish to go through the IRS and Circuit Courts waving reports of this case around, you can, but it's a time-consuming, costly procedure and will not guarantee that you'll win *your* case.

BUSINESS TELEPHONE CALLS

A separate phone for business would be ideal because it would be an uncomplicated matter to deduct the entire cost at the end of the year. If this is not possible, keep a careful record of your long distance telephone calls made for business reasons. I simply type out a sheet as shown below. It specifies the year, the date, who was called, the city, the state, the phone number, the reason for the call, and the cost. I fill in most of the information after I make the call and then, after receiving my monthly bill, I sit down and enter the costs.

YEAR _____

LONG DISTANCE PHONE CALLS

DATE	NAME&COMPANY	CITY/STATE	NUMBER	REASON	AMOUNT

Your accountant will also allocate part of the monthly service charge, which would represent the business use of the phone.

And! Don't forget that every dime you deposit calling your service or machine from the outside should be notated in your journal, as they are deductible. These "necessary nickels" can add up to a few dollars a week, and almost $150.00 per year. (Don't forget long distance calls to retrieve any messages when you are out of town.) It's again a good idea to attach a supporting schedule that reads "OUTSIDE PHONE CALLS—$3.00 a week; $3.00x50 = $150.00.

DEPRECIATION OF EQUIPMENT

Should you buy a musical instrument, typewriter, car, computer, desk, filing cabinet, tape recorder, answering machine, etc., you would not deduct the total cost of the piece of equipment in a lump sum in one tax year. Instead, you would "depreciate" the cost by deducting a fraction of it over several years—thus spreading the deduction over the "useful life" of the item.

There are three methods of depreciation: Straight line, Accelerated Cost Recovery System (ACRS) and First Year Expensing. Depending on your expectations of earnings in the next five years, your accountant will decide which method of depreciation will do you the most good.

GETTING AROUND TOWN

A self-employed professional may deduct transportation costs necessary to work—car and public transportation expenses to and from meetings, rehearsals, lessons, and business errands. If you work at home, you can deduct the cost of getting to your first business appointment of the day and all other business-related transportation costs. But, if you work at an office and later cab it over to an audition or rehearsal, the audition/rehearsal traveling cost is deductible but the cost of getting to the office in the morning is not. If you are an employed professional and must go to daily orchestra or opera rehearsals and performances, the regular, daily commuting expenses are *not* deductible. However, if you travel to an audition or freelance job or go on a musical errand later that day, the costs *are* deductible.

Auto

You have a choice here. You can either deduct the actual operating expenses of your car for business purposes (gas, oil, insurance, repairs, tolls, and parking), or you can deduct a flat allowance. In addition to the allowance, you may claim parking, tolls, and interest expenses for the car. Check with your accountant. The allowance, though, is generous and definitely more convenient. It also includes depreciation.

ON THE ROAD AGAIN

If you must travel out of town for your work, you can deduct the ordinary and necessary travel expenses on all working days. You can also deduct expenses for weekends and holidays that interrupt your work time. If your trip is part business, part pleasure, you can deduct only for the portion of your expenses allocable to business activities. Should you wish to deduct all the transportation expenses of this "semi-business trip," then you must have initiated the trip primarily for business reasons and the travel must be confined within the United States. Should you travel outside the United States for more than a week and you spend 25 percent (or more) of your time on nonbusiness activities, you would have to allocate part of your transportation costs to the personal part of the trip. Make notations in your diary as to the day of departure and return, destinations, etc. Save all ticket stubs, receipts, and any canceled checks.

Travel to foreign conferences or conventions has strict limitations regarding deductions. (No doubt the convention sponsors would know the story.) Study IRS publication #463 to prep yourself on travel deductions.

Now, your food and lodging are totally deductible but the records here are especially important. The bills for hotels and restaurants must show the name of the establishment, its address, the date, and an itemized list of the expenses. Tips, baggage checks, telephone, and laundry outlays are deductible, and a diary entry is sufficient substantiation.

Note: If you are considered an employee in a company or orchestra and you must travel for business, you can only deduct the costs of transportation, room, and board if you are expected to pay for them out of your own salary. These figures are entered on Form 2106, Part I.

PER DIEM

A *per diem* is an allowance from your employer (from which no taxes are withheld) to cover food, lodging and laundry expenses while you are away from home and on the job. If you've ever toured, the phrase "per diem" comes quickly to the tongue. As of this writing, the IRS states that per diems need not be reported as income if they do not exceed $50.00 per day. If you find that your reasonable expenses (hotels, food, tips, etc.) exceed your per diem, you are allowed to exclude the per diem from taxes and also deduct the excess on Form 2106.

All of this will need careful "combing through" by your accountant; if you keep very accurate records and receipts of your per diems and expenses, it can be handled at tax time.

INTEREST

The interest on business loans, personal loans, credit cards, and department store bills is deductible. If the interest payments were on business items or loans, they are deductible and entered on Schedule C. If they are personal, they are deductible on Schedule A if you itemize. (See Nonbusiness Deductions.)

THE SELF-EMPLOYMENT TAX

A self-employed artist doesn't have an employer to withhold Social Security from his salary. Thus, Schedule SE is used to compute this tax. This form must be filed if your net self-employment income is $400.00 or greater, after you have taken all your business deductions.

NONBUSINESS DEDUCTIONS

No matter what your employment category, you can take deductions for certain nonbusiness expenses. These are entered on Schedule A of the 1040 Form *only if you itemize!* When you itemize, you list certain deductible expenses connected with your nonbusiness life. You can do this only if your total itemized deductions are greater than the standard deduction (called the zero bracket amount). There are different standard amounts depending on your filing status:

Married, joint—	$3,400
Married, filing separately—	$1,700
(Note: If your spouse itemizes, you must itemize also.)	
Single—	$2,300

If you itemize on Schedule A you may deduct the following expenses:

Medical and Dental Expenses: You can deduct that portion of your medical and dental expenses which exceeds 5 percent of your adjusted gross income as entered on Form 1040. You may include the cost of transportation to and from the doctor's office as part of medical and dental expenses.

The following is a partial list of medical deductions. It is neither definitive nor exhaustive and is subject to change:

Professional Services:	All fees paid to medical professionals including chiropractors, Christian Science Practitioners, and registered nurses
Dental Services:	Teeth cleaning Extractions Fillings Gum Treatments Orthodonture Oral Surgery X-rays
Equipment:	Air conditioner (only if prescribed for allergies) Ambulance Braces and crutches Eyeglasses and contact lenses Special mattress and bedboards
Treatment:	Acupuncture Injections Lab tests Pre- and postnatal treatments Psychotherapy
Medicines:	Prescriptions Prescribed vitamins

Beginning in 1984, the 1 percent of adjusted gross income limit on drugs is eliminated. However, the deduction on drugs will be allowed only for prescription drugs and insulin.

Charitable Contributions

If you contribute to a tax-exempt organization, you may take a deduction even if you don't itemize on Schedule A. You enter the amount on Form 1040 but it is limited to 25 percent of the first $300.00 contributed. This percentage is escalating so check on it from year to year.

If you are a volunteer in an organization, you may not deduct the estimated value of your time and services, but you are allowed to deduct taxis or supplies. There is also a nine cents allowance for the operations of your car while doing volunteer work. Make a note of the times you do volunteer and distances to the organization if you drive and, of course, write down cab fares in your journal.

When you give away clothing, books, etc. to a tax-exempt organization, get a receipt with the organization's name and a description of what's been donated. You may claim the fair market value of that property.

Also Deductible on Schedule A if You Itemize

    Health insurance premiums
    Casualty or theft losses
    State sales tax
    Home mortgages
    Interest on personal loans, credit cards, and charge accounts
    Personal accounting and tax preparation fees
    Political contributions (up to $100.00)

WHAT IS UNEARNED INCOME?

Some grants, dividends, interest, royalties, alimony, unemployment, and debt cancellation are considered unearned income. These different kinds of income will be accounted for on different forms.

Grants and Prizes:

You may exclude from your tax computations up to $300.00 per month from qualifying grants for a maximum of thirty-six months in your lifetime. Your grantor will inform you as to the tax status of your grant.

Prizes or awards you win, but for which you did not apply, are not taxed.

Dividends and Interest:	Unless they derive from a tax-exempt source (such as Federal and Municipal bonds) dividends are taxable. If you earn $400 or less, it is entered on Form 1040. Over $400 is entered on Schedule B, Part I. This holds true for interest, also. Everyone is entitled to a $100 exclusion on dividends. However you must report it.
Royalties:	Royalties from books, compositions, etc. go on Schedule E, Part I. Royalties from ongoing employment go on Residual Form 1040.
State and Local Tax Refunds:	State and city taxes can be deducted from your Federal taxes. However, if you get a refund later, it must be declared as income the following year if you itemized. This category is entered on Form 1040.
Debt Cancellation:	A cancellation of a debt is counted as income as it "enriches" the debtor because it does away with the obligation to pay. If, however, the debt is canceled as a gift, you don't have to report the canceled amount.
Alimony:	Alimony is taxable income, but your accountant will check the laws for you. Child support is *not* taxable.
Unemployment:	Unemployment money is taxable if your total income from wages interest, dividends, and unemployment amounts to more than $12,000 for a single person or $18,000 for a married couple filing jointly. If you are married and living with your spouse but file separately, all of your unemployment may be taxed.

Untaxed Income
    Interest from municipal bonds
    Workers' Compensation
    Disability Benefits
    Child Support
    Certain grants and prizes

WHO MUST FILE?

If you are single and your gross income is less than $3,300 or you are married and your combined gross income is less than $5,400, you don't have to file a tax return. You *must* file if you want to get back your withholdings—the portion of your salary that was withheld for taxes by your employer. Also, if you are self-employed and had net earnings of $400 or more during the year, you must file. If you are claimed as a dependent on someone else's return and you received $1,000 or more from unearned income (e.g. interest, grants, unemployment, etc.) you must file. Note, however, that this is in reference to unearned income here.

    You should file even if you are not required to. The reason for this? Well, you may not be making much money now, but should your income increase significantly in a future year, you can *income average*. This is a method of calculation that takes into account your past poverty. If you have a "feast" year and the four years before were definitely from hunger (and you have the returns to substantiate this), you can take an average of the previous four years' earnings plus this year's and nestle into a lower tax bracket, thus saving yourself a lot of money. You file Schedule G to average and you must have copies of your tax returns for the preceding four years. If you can't hunt them up, call the person who prepared them to check if they're on file, or contact the IRS Center nearest to you and they will forward copies (so slowly that you'd best think ahead and make that call fast).

APPROACHING APRIL 15

No matter how many math courses you aced, I don't advise you to do your returns yourself. I *do* advise you to seek a tax consultant who specializes in your artistic field as he or she will understand the fine points and be familiar with the IRS's difficulties with some of our professional deductions. Did you know that in the entire Internal Revenue Code Book there is not even a listing or reference to the profession "Actor" or "Actress"? Taking this into consideration, a specialist will explicitly prepare your return, and don't forget that he or she is in a position to give advice and guidance and point out yearly changes in the tax structure to you.

Check trade newspapers or call your local Arts Council or professional associations to get a recommendation for a good accountant. Then, once you link up, prepare very carefully for your appointment. The more organized you are, the more quality time he or she can devote to your situation. This will undoubtedly lead to your getting back or keeping more money. Make an appointment as early as possible; April (and the weeks preceding it) *is* the cruelest month and a harried accountant will do the job, but won't be able to give it an optimum focusing in.

After taking the history of your financial year and gathering up your W2's, totals of expenses, statements of interest etc., your accountant will prepare your Federal and State/City tax returns.

Each return *must* be signed. If you forget to add your signature, the IRS will consider it as unfiled. If you're filing a joint return, you and your spouse must sign both forms.

Then, if you owe any taxes, the money is due with the return. Staple the check right on it and mail the return to the Service Center named in the Form 1040 directions *no later than April 15.* The postmark on the envelope will be treated as the filing date, so if you mail very close to April 15th, get your envelope stamped with a date at the post office.

Should you need an extension of time to prepare your return, request it *by April 15* on Form 4868. Please note that you must pay the total tax due on or before April 15th. If you don't include an estimated payment with the extension request, it will be as though you never requested it. Be careful; if you underestimate by more than 10 percent you may have to pay a penalty. The extension is for a four-month period.

WHAT IF YOU CAN'T PAY?

I was at a party and heard a distressing story. A musician who hadn't figured her tax assessment would be much at all, found out that she owed the government $400.00. She got panicky and, not knowing what to do, she turned around and sold a $1500 flute for the sum she needed to mail in. *This should never have happened!*

If you legitimately cannot afford to pay your taxes, you file the return without the check, but attach a letter explaining that you're having financial difficulties at this time. The IRS will contact you and send you a bill. At this point, you should visit the IRS office nearest you and arrange a meeting. You can obtain an extension of time by showing evidence of financial hardship on Form 1127. Interest will be charged on the unpaid balance, but you and the IRS will work out an equitable payment arrangement. Try not to think of the IRS as a fiendish enemy.

What Happens Then?

Once your return is received at the Service Center it will be examined for correctness. The math will be checked first and a mistake in either direction will bring you a bill or a refund.

Some returns are looked at more closely. If you're going to be audited, you'll receive (unhappily no doubt) a letter in the mail. Sometimes only a part of your return, such as medical expenses, is considered in the audit.

If you've kept really good records and honestly filed the information, there is no reason to get upset over an audit. It is a meeting and examination of your assertions and it's possible that it will be more of an educational session for the examiner. Try not to become paranoid.

If deductions are disallowed and you agree to the agent's assessment of additional taxes, you will be asked to sign Form 870. This form is, in effect, an agreement that you are not going to appeal the decision. If you disagree and want to take the matter further, you have a set period of time in which to file an appeal.

ESTIMATED TAXES

I always thought April 15th was "the tax season." Well, it is. But so is June 15th, September 15th, and January 15th. You see, taxes are withheld from employees on an ongoing basis and for the self-employed through estimated taxes on Form 1040-ES.

You figure out what you owe by looking at last year's total tax situation. Then, you make quarterly payments and still file a Form 1040 on or before April 15th. On the Form 1040, you compute the difference between what you have already paid and your total tax liability. If you paid more than you really owe, you will either be mailed a refund or you can apply to have the overpayment credited to next year's taxes.

You must file a 1040-ES if your estimated tax balance due is $400.00 or more and either your gross income includes more than $500.00 from sources other than wages subject to withholding or your salary and wage income exceeds $20,000.00.

What If I Just Learned of a Deduction I Didn't Take?

You can file an amendment for up to three years to add a deduction you forgot to take (or didn't know was allowed). You do this by filing Form

1040X with an amended Schedule C if it was a business deduction, amended Schedule A if it was a nonbusiness deduction or amended Schedule G if you now decide to income average.

There! That wasn't *so* terrible, I hope. It's mostly a matter of a new vocabulary and a lot of formidable-sounding forms and categories. Don't be put off if you're not quite comfortable with words like "depreciation" or "income averaging." It's more important that you keep accurate records, journal entries, receipts, and canceled checks. If the picture is clear, a good accountant will pull everything together and see that it lands on the right forms. If you'd like to read about your tax situation in more depth, I urge you to purchase a copy of *Fear of Filing* by Volunteer Lawyers for the Arts (see Appendices). It's comprehensive and extremely helpful.

Little by little, you'll become familiar with the whys and wherefores and begin to work through this system with aplomb. Oh, by the way—did you enter the purchase price of this book in your journal and financial sheet and put the receipt away? J-U-S-T C-H-E-C-K-I-N-G!

Afterword

I HOPE THIS BOOK has been a help to you, and that you understand the merchandising techniques which will highlight your talents and organize your life as a professional. I'd like to close with a few thoughts about this thing called a career in music.

We all have our dreams, and fulfilling them is important. But keep in mind that reality is made of different stuff from fantasy. Try to remain flexible and don't be afraid to adjust and adapt your career goals as you recognize the realities.

Work hard, do your homework, and continue to stretch for new standards of excellence, but not at the expense of other dimensions of your personality and intellect. A mind that is active and enriched is much more creative and exciting.

You'll find that each career has its own individual rhyme and reason and that fame and fortune are not often the measuring sticks of success. For me, the people I've met, the places I've seen, and the growth I've experienced are the truly lasting payoffs.

Moreover, the energy, discipline, and determination it took to decode the musical system and rise to performance levels tempered me for other aspects of life. People often grimace and ask me if I don't find writing terribly difficult. I understand what they're driving at, but—after memorizing hundreds of pages in many different languages, walking onto a stage and connecting with an audience, conductor, and orchestra (all the while striving for musical, technical, and theatrical accuracy)—putting down some thoughts in my own language doesn't strike me as impossible! There are some nice side effects as a result of our kind of training. Be on the lookout for them and don't underestimate your considerable accomplishments.

And never forget that two hands brought enthusiastically together after a performance in a small-town auditorium are as meaningful as two applauding at the Met. *Move* people with your music.

APPENDICES

JOB SPECIFICATION SHEET

DATE: _____

TIME: _____

ORGANIZATION: _____

_____

_____

_____

PHONE: (_____) _____

CONTACT: _____

REFERRED BY: _____

FEE: _____ DISTRIBUTION: _____

AGENT'S FEE: _____

LENGTH OF PROGRAM: _____

PROGRAM REQUESTS: _____

_____

_____

_____

SIZE OF AUDITORIUM: _____ PHYSICAL CHAR-

ACTERISTICS:

_____

_____

AUDIO SYSTEM? _____

MUSIC STANDS? _____

MODE OF TRANSPORTATION: _____ COST: _____

DIRECTIONS: _____

_____

_____

_____

AFTERNOTES: _____

_____

_____

_____

SIZE OF AUDIENCE: _____

   This simple sheet put an end to my "Scattered-about-the-House" Syndrome. I used to write down information on a lot of different pieces of paper and drove myself crazy trying to locate everything. Now, as soon as I get a job, I fill out this sheet with all the specifics, staple the contract and program to it, and keep it filed in a folder marked "JOBS."

   Later I refer to the sheets to remind me of fee quotes, programs, program lengths, etc.

A "PERFORMANCE CHECKLIST"

I remember sitting down on the floor two hours before my first important recital, intently wrapping a gift for my accompanist. A day after the event, I noticed I'd cut through the wires of my stereo as well as the wrapping paper! This was a pretty strong clue that I wasn't to be trusted for much right before a performance. Therefore, I devised this checklist for my own protection and peace of mind.

A week before an engagement, I take out a photocopy of the list of paraphernalia I normally haul along to a performance site, and circle in red the items I'll need (of course, I add on anything specific). This gives me time to purchase any needed supplies. Two days before the concert, I lay out the items on the list. Then, the day of the performance, I pack up with another, less nervous partner, who checks off the list as the items disappear into the bag.

This way, I never close the door and worry that I've forgotten anything. Devise your own idiosyncratic list, photocopy it, and keep a supply on hand in a folder. It works!

SAMPLE PERFORMANCE CHECKLIST

Concert Apparel
Shoes
Stockings
Instrument(s)
Music Stand
Music
Business Cards/Brochures
Programs/Translations
Lightweight Steamer
Emergency Sewing Repair Kit
Earrings/Jewelry
Checkbook
Cash
Medications
Contacts/Solution/Emergency Set of Glasses
Extra Strings/Reeds etc.
Clothespins (to hold music if concert is out of doors)

Toothbrush/Toothpaste
Camera/Flash/Film
Tape Recorder/Tapes
Thermos of Tea and Lemon
Makeup
Hair Spray/Bobby Pins

MAINTAINING A PERSONAL MAILING LIST

All musicians need to build a following and inform others of their artistic involvements. Therefore, it is never too soon to compile a personal mailing list. If you set it up and maintain it through the years, it will be invaluable to you for your announcements and you can trade it for the lists of friends and organizations.

The most efficient and economical way to keep your list is to purchase a packet of self-adhesive (pressure-sensitive) address labels. You can find them at any stationery supply store. They are 1x2¾ inch labels, thirty-three on an 8½x11 sheet.

A typing guide is included with the sheets and you simply place it underneath a piece of bond (typing) paper. Then you type the name and address within the confines of the label guide. The bond paper becomes your master list. You take the masters and the blank label sheets to a photocopy store and have the master list copied right onto the labels. This way, you eliminate repeat typing. Note: some photocopy stores stock these blank label sheets; inquire so you'll know.

I code my list with my initials on the lower right hand corner so I know it's my personal group of friends and relatives. Other compilations I code with any system that makes sense to me—i.e., *cp:* concert presenters; *mg:* management firms; etc. The code makes it easy to isolate labels for specific mailings and locate labels for deletions or address changes. Don't neglect to update your list; why waste the time, paper, and postage on future mailings?

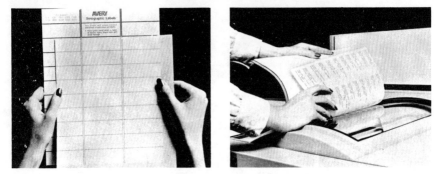

Photographs courtesy of Avery Label
Your mailing list need be typed only once if you use a typing guide to type a master. The self-adhesive labels can be loaded into a photocopy machine, and the names and addresses are copied from the master onto the labels.

STATIONERY SPECIFICATIONS

The letterhead stationery in this book was specified to the typesetter as follows:*

Barbara Solomon:	36 point Goudy Bold
	10 point Helvetica
Cameron Taylor:	30 point Mistral (Prestype)
	10 point Oracle
Terry Slavin:	30 point Eras Heavy
	10 Point Eras Book
Delos String Quartet:	30 point American Classic Bold
	10 point American Classic Regular
Doberman Beach Concerts:	26 point Tiffany Demi Bold
	10 point Megaron Medium
Paul Bogdasarian:	36 point Broadway
	8 point Megaron Medium
Covington String Quartet:	36 point Eras Demi Bold
	10 point Eras Medium

*The larger point size specifies the setting of the name, the smaller specifies the address.

SERVICES

THE AMERICAN MUSIC CENTER

In March of 1939, five composers (Otto Luening, Quincy Porter, Aaron Copland, Howard Hanson, and Marion Bauer) met at Aaron Copland's 63rd Street studio in New York City in order to incorporate as the American Music Center. They felt that American music acutely needed an archive and distribution center.

Today, the membership of this nonprofit organization includes composers, performers, critics, and patrons of American music as well as publishers, recording companies, and institutions. The office at 250 West 54th Street has a comprehensive music library and research center where composers, performers, and researchers can find scores, recordings, videotapes, and information on the practical side of composing.

Composers from all over the nation can send in their scores and publicize the fact of their existence through the Research Libraries Information Network. Performers can peruse AMC's catalogues at computer terminals in libraries around the country and borrow scores through a system of inter-library loans.

Every week over two hundred questions are answered by the AMC staff, who provide information on publishing and recording, on performing groups and on how to obtain performances, on copyrights and royalties, and on available grants and fellowships. Ensembles can learn about the commissioning process and can obtain information about funding available for the performance of new music. The AMC also cooperates with performers and performing organizations to help them find repertoires suitable for their audiences and works with them to increase their ability to promote and publicize performance of new music.

The *AMC Newsletter* informs members of competitions and grants and offers much helpful information.

Contact: American Music Center, Inc., 250 West 54th Street, New York NY 10019, (212)247-3121.

CENTER FOR ARTS INFORMATION

The Center for Arts Information was established in 1976 as the first comprehensive, cross-disciplinary information clearinghouse and management assistance center for the nonprofit arts. This organization serves artists and arts administrators by maintaining a six-thousand-volume research library, funding publications relevant to the artist, and offering information referral to the approximately 10,000 people who call, write, or visit each year.

Some of the library information is collected according to subject areas such as audience development, competitions and commissions, festivals, financial management, fundraising, marketing, public relations, vocational guidance, and workshops and classes.

The following is a sampling of questions the staff can answer:

- "Where can I get a good press list for my concert announcement?"

- "I need to videotape a performance. Do you know where I could get a video artist at a low cost?"

- "Where can I get legal assistance on a copyright problem?"

- "Where can I get free help in setting up my bookkeeping system?"

- "Where can I get an emergency loan?"

- "What publications feature arts employment listings?"

If you have these or any other arts-related questions, write, call or visit (the library is open to the public by appointment only): The Center for Arts Information, 625 Broadway, New York NY 10012. (212)677-7548.

CENTRAL OPERA SERVICE

The Central Opera Service (COS) was established in 1954 to foster a closer association among civic, community, college, and national opera companies throughout the country, to assist them in reaching ever higher artistic standards, and thus to encourage national interest in and enthusiasm for opera.

Central Opera Service has become the nation's leading and most respected source for information on all aspects of opera and serves its members as well as national arts organizations by providing information related to repertory, production, scores, translations, scenery, costumes, and budgets. Extensive up-to-date files on every aspect of opera are maintained for this purpose. The Service also maintains the most comprehensive operatic archives (thirty thousand operas and musical theater pieces) in the United States.

Singers would be particularly interested in COS's publication, "Career Guide for the Young American Singer," which lists national and international competitions, grants for study, apprentice programs, and statements on auditions and hiring policies by major American opera companies. Also, take a look at the "Directory of Opera/Musical Theatre Companies and Workshops in the U.S. and Canada," which is a current listing of addresses for approximately eleven hundred producing organizations. Self-adhesive mailing labels for this list are also available.

Contact: Central Opera Service, Metropolitan Opera—Lincoln Center, New York NY 10023, (212)799-3467.

CHAMBER MUSIC AMERICA

Chamber music is thriving in this nation, and a lot of credit should go to an organization called Chamber Music America. Chamber Music America was founded in 1977 to "provide a unifying umbrella for professional chamber musicians to enable them to strengthen their voice in gaining government support and to promote the welfare of professional ensembles across the country."

In 1980, with a lot of CMA urging, the National Endowment of the Arts established a direct chamber music funding program. Since then the Endowment has provided close to 2 million dollars in direct grants to ensembles and presenters.

Chamber Music America's membership includes managers, music businesses, and training programs, as well as professional ensembles and concert presenters. The organization provides its members with direct grants for residencies and composition, a referral and consultation service, health insurance, and low-cost instrument coverage. There are two national conventions each year and CMA's quarterly publication, *Chamber Music Magazine* (formerly *American Ensemble*), is one of the few magazines that tackle the real-life concerns of the professional musician. Little hype, lots of help.

Get in touch with Chamber Music America, 215 Park Avenue South, New York, NY 10003. (212)460-9030.

COMPUTERS FOR THE ARTS

If you have an ensemble in Cincinnati and you want to send a typed, personalized letter to every concert presenter, arts council, and foundation within a 400-mile radius, would you:

1. Try to collect a list of names and addresses (praying that they are up to date) and type and address every one yourself?

OR

2. Call Computers for the Arts?

If you want to give your New York debut and you wish to do a bulk rate mailing to a Contemporary, Early Music, or Chamber Music audience list, would you:

- Hire someone to purchase a list for you and hope that you sort and bundle it according to U.S. Postal specifications?

OR

- Call Computers for the Arts?

If you circled 2 *twice*, you can congratulate yourself! You are a State-of-the-Art Musician. You can put computers to work for you.

Computers for the Arts has national services geared toward classical artists and artists' managements. They can computerize your list and put it in ZIP code order, and they can augment your list by merging it with theirs (purging the result of any duplications). They also offer a unique bulk mail program. Your lists are printed out in the proper order for post office bundling complete with foolproof instructions and stickers. (See Chapter 6 to truly appreciate this service.) If you like, they will handle your entire mailing. You send over the flyers and they will generate labels, affix them, sort, bundle, and sack and deliver the sacks to the post office. There is no minimum order and phone and office consultations are welcomed.

Computers for the Arts is run by performers who face the same problems as you—but they overcome them with the use of a computer.

Contact: Computers for the Arts, 945 West End Ave., Suite 1C, New York NY 10025. (212)222-0085.

MEET THE COMPOSER

Meet the Composer is a national service organization whose purpose is to bring together living composers with audiences. This is accomplished by granting financial assistance to support the composer's fee for events at which the composer's music and presence are featured. Since 1974, some twenty-six thousand Meet the Composer events have reached over 13 million people. More than forty-four hundred new works have been commissioned and premiered.

Any nonprofit, tax-exempt organization wishing to invite a composer may apply, and all composers are eligible for consideration. (Note: Events and compositions may range from traditional concert music to folk, jazz and experimental.) The important ingredient is exchange between the composer and the audience, so the composer must participate in the event. He or she may perform, conduct, speak, present a workshop, or be interviewed on radio or TV.

So, if a nonprofit quartet in Colorado wanted to create a real event for an audience, the media, themselves, and contemporary music, they could choose a composer (MTC staff will recommend appropriate candidates) and bring him or her to the concert hall or "new performance space" with the assistance of a Meet the Composer grant. The event would no doubt boost ticket sales and critical attention, the performers would add a personalized work to their repertoire *and*, the composer gains visibility, encouragement, and financial compensation to continue working and contributing to American music.

For more information contact:

Meet the Composer (National Office)
250 W. 57th St., Suite 2532
New York NY 10107
(212)247-4082

Meet the Composer New England
Erika Zaccardo
c/o The New England Foundation for the Arts
25 Mount Auburn St.
Cambridge MA 02138
(617)492-2914
(serves Connecticut, Massachusetts, Rhode Island, Vermont, and New Hampshire)

Michael Braun
Affiliate State Arts Agencies of the Upper Midwest
528 Hennetin Ave. #204
Minneapolis MN 55403
(serves Iowa, Minnesota, North and South Dakota)

Meet the Composer Great Lakes
Hedy Pufeles Milgrom
Great Lakes Arts Alliance
11424 Bellflower Rd.
Cleveland OH 44106
(216)229-1098
(serves Illinois, Indiana, Michigan, and Ohio)

Meet the Composer California
Carl Stone
849 S. Broadway, Suite 639
Los Angeles CA 90014
(213)623-1122

Meet the Composer Texas
Tara Elgin Holley
Austin Music Umbrella
Box 1438
Austin TX 78767
(512)476-1324

VOLUNTEER LAWYERS FOR THE ARTS

Volunteer Lawyers for the Arts (VLA) arranges for free legal representation and counseling and provides legal education to the arts community. Artists and nonprofit arts organizations with arts-related legal problems who are unable to afford private counsel are eligible for VLA's assistance.

Legal matters handled by VLA must be directly related to the practice of one's art. These include such matters as:

- Contracts
- Copyright
- Incorporation and tax exemption
- Labor relations
- Insurance
- Loft problems

- Small claims court advice

- General corporate

VLA's publications and communications programs attempt to educate artists and attorneys about the kinds of legal problems artists and arts organizations face and to familiarize them with available solutions. VLA is a nonprofit, tax-exempt corporation supported by the National Endowment for the Arts, the New York State Council on the Arts, individual contributions, private foundations, and corporations.

For more information and a list of regional Volunteer Lawyers for the Arts groups, contact: Volunteer Lawyers for the Arts, 1560 Broadway, Suite 711, New York NY 10036. (212)575-1150.

STATE ARTS COUNCILS

Alabama State Council on the Arts & Humanities
Gallagher House
114 North Hull St.
Montgomery AL 36130
(205)832-6758

Alaska State Council on the Arts
619 Warehouse Ave., Suite ™220
Anchorage AK 99501
(9078)279-1558

American Samoa Council on Culture, Arts, & Humanities
Box 1540
Office of the Governor
Pago Pago AS 96799
9-011-684-633-5613
9-011-684-633-4347

Arizona Commission on the Arts & Humanities
2024 N. Seventh St., Suite #201
Phoenix AZ 85006
(602)255-5884 (office)

Arkansas Arts Council
Continental Building, Suite #500
Main and Markham St.
Little Rock AR 72201
(501)371-2539

California Arts Council
1901 Broadway, Suite A
Sacramento CA 95818
(916)445-1530

Colorado Council on the Arts & Humanities
Grant-Humphreys Mansion
770 Pennsylvania St.
Denver, CO 80203
(303)866-2617/8

Connecticut Commission on the Arts
340 Capital Ave.
Hartford CN 06106
(203)566-4770

Delaware State Arts Council
State Office Building
820 N. French St.
Wilmington DE 19801
(302)571-3540

District of Columbia Commission on The Arts & Humanities
420 Seventh St., NW, 2nd Floor
Washington DC 20004
(202)724-5613
(202)727-9332

Arts Council of Florida
Division of Cultural Affairs
Department of State
The Capitol
Tallahassee FL 32301
(904)487-2980

Georgia Council for the Arts & Humanities
Suite 100
2082 East Exchange Pl.
Tucker GA 30084
(404)656-3967

Guam Council on the Arts & Humanities
Office of the Governor
Box 2950
Agana GU 96910

State Foundation on Culture & The Arts (Hawaii)
335 Merchant St., Rm. #202
Honolulu HI 96813
(808)548-4145

Idaho Commission on the Arts
304 W. State St.
c/o Statehouse
Boise ID 83720
(208)334-2119

Illinois Arts Council
111 North Wabash Ave., Rm. 720
Chicago IL 60602
(312)793-6750

Indiana Arts Commission
Union Title Bldg., Suite 614
155 East Market St.
Indianapolis IN 46204
(317)232-1268

Iowa State Arts Council
State Capital Bldg.
Des Moines IA 50319
(515)281-4451

Kansas Arts Commission
112 W. 6th St.
Topeka KS 66603
(913)296-3335

Kentucky Arts Council
Berry Hill
Louisville Rd.
Frankfort KY 40601
(502)564-3757

Department of Culture, Recreation, & Tourism
Division of Arts
Box 44247
Baton Rouge LA 70804
(504)925-3930

Maine State Commission on the Arts & the Humanities
55 Capitol St.
State House Station 25
Augusta ME 04333
(207)289-2724

Maryland State Arts Council
15 West Mulberry St.
Baltimore MD 21201
(301)685-6740

Massachusetts Council on The Arts & Humanities
1 Ashburton Pl., Rm. 2101
Boston MA 02108
(617)727-3668

Michigan Council for the Arts
1200 Sixth Ave.
Executive Plaza
Detroit MI 48226
(313)256-3735

Minnesota State Arts Board
432 Summit Ave.
St. Paul MN 55102
(612)297-2603
(800)652-9747—toll free within Minnesota

Mississippi Arts Commission
301 N. Lamar St. (site)
Box 1341 (mailing address)
Jackson MS 39205
(601)354-7336

Missouri State Council on the Arts
Wainwright State Office Complex
111 N. Seventh St., Suite 105
St. Louis MO 63101
(314)444-6854

Montana Arts Council
1280 S. Third St. West
Missoula MT 59801
(406)543-8286

Nebraska Arts Council
1313 Farnam-on-the-Mall
Omaha NB 68102-1873
(402)554-2122

Nevada State Council on the Arts
329 Flint St.
Reno NV 89501
(702)789-0225

New Hampshire Commission on the Arts
Phenix Hall
40 N. Main St.
Concord NH 03301
(603)271-2789

New Jersey State Council on the Arts
109 W. State St.
Trenton NJ 08608
(609)292-6130

New Mexico Arts Division
224 E. Palace Ave.
Santa Fe NM 87501
(505)827-6490

New York State Council on the Arts
80 Centre St.
New York NY 10013
(212)587-4555

North Carolina Arts Council
N.C. Dept. of Cultural Resources
Raleigh NC 27611
(919)733-2821

North Dakota Council on the Arts
Black Building, Suite 811
Fargo ND 58102
(701)237-8962

Commonwealth Council for Arts & Culture
(Northern Mariana Islands)
Ferreira Bldg., Beach Rd.
Garapan, Saipan
Commonwealth of the Northern Mariana Islands 96950

Ohio Arts Council
727 E. Main St.
Columbus OH 43205
(614)466-2613

State Arts Council of Oklahoma
Jim Thorpe Building, Rm. #640
2101 N. Lincoln Blvd.
Oklahoma City OK 73105
(405)521-2931

Oregon Arts Commission
835 Summer St., N.E.
Salem OR 97301
(503)378-3625

Commonwealth of Pennsylvania Council on the Arts
Rm. 216, Finance Bldg.
Harrisburg PA 17120
(717)787-6883

Institute of Puerto Rican Culture
Apartado Postal 4184
San Juan PR 00905
(809)723-2115

Rhode Island State Council on the Arts
312 Wickenden St.
Providence RI 02903-4494
(401)277-3880

South Carolina Arts Commission
1800 Gervais St.
Columbia SC 29201
(803)758-3442

South Dakota Arts Council
108 W. 11th St.
Sioux Falls SD 57102
(605)339-6646

Tennessee Arts Commission
505 Deaderick St., Suite 1700
Nashville TN 37219
(615)741-6395 (office)
(615)741-1701 (switchboard)

Texas Commission on the Arts
Box 13406
Capitol Station
Austin TX 78711
(512)475-6593

Utah Arts Council
617 E. South Temple St.
Salt Lake City UT 84102
(801)533-5895/6

Vermont Council on the Arts, Inc.
136 State St.
Montpelier VT 05602
(802)828-3291

Virginia Commission for the Arts
400 E. Grace St., First Floor
Richmond VA 23219
(804)786-4492

Virgin Islands Council on the Arts
Caravelle Arcade
Christiansted, St. Croix
U.S. VI 00820
(809)773-3075 ext. 3

Box 103
St. Thomas VI 00801
(809)774-5984

Washington State Arts Commission
9th and Columbia Bldg.
Mail Stop GH-11
Olympia WA 98504
(206)753-3860

Arts & Humanities Division
West Virginia Department of Culture and History
Science & Culture Center
Capitol Complex
Charleston WV 25305
(304)348-0240

Wisconsin Arts Board
123 W. Washington Ave.
Madison WI 53702
(608)266-0190

Wyoming Council on the Arts
Equality State Bank Bldg.
2nd Floor
Cheyenne WY 82002
(307)777-7742

REGIONAL ARTS ORGANIZATIONS

Affiliated State Arts Agencies of the Upper Midwest
Hennepin Center for the Arts
528 Hennepin Ave., Suite 302
Minneapolis MN 55403
(612)341-0755

(serves North Dakota, Minnesota, South Dakota, Wisconsin,
Iowa)

Consortium for Pacific Arts & Cultures
Box 4204
Honolulu HI 96813
(808)524-6128

(serves Alaska, Hawaii, California, Guam, American Samoa,
Northern Marianas)

Great Lakes Arts Alliance
11424 Bellflower Rd.
Cleveland OH 44106
(216)229-1098

(serves Ohio, Michigan, Indiana, Illinois)

Mid America Arts Alliance
20 West 9th St., Suite 550
Kansas City MO 64105
(816)421-1388

(serves Nebraska, Kansas, Oklahoma, Missouri, Arkansas, Texas*)
(*Associate Member)

Mid Atlantic States Arts Consortium, Inc.
Suite 7-B
11 E. Chase St.
Baltimore MD 21202
(301)685-1400

(serves New York, Pennsylvania, New Jersey, Maryland, Delaware, West Virginia, District of Columbia, Virginia)

New England Foundation for the Arts, Inc.
25 Mount Auburn St.
Cambridge MA 02138
(617)492-2914

(serves Connecticut, Maine, Massachusetts, New Hampshire, Rhode Island, Vermont)

Southern Arts Federation
1401 Peachtree Street, N.E., Suit #122
Atlanta GA 30309
(404)874-7244

(serves Alabama, Florida, Georgia, Kentucky, Mississippi, Louisiana, North Carolina, Tennessee, South Carolina)

Western States Arts Foundation
141 E. Palace Ave.
Santa Fe NM 87501
(505)988-1166

(serves Washington, Oregon, Utah, Montana, Idaho, Wyoming, Nevada, Colorado, Arizona, New Mexico)

NOTES ON NOT-FOR-PROFIT

Here and there throughout the book, I've mentioned the phrase "not-for-profit" in situations which seem to suggest that the not-for-profit ensemble is the fairest of them all. These types of ensembles are eligible for a lower bulk rate fee, Public Service Announcements, Meet the Composer grants and, as you'll soon see, the not-for-profit ensemble is more likely to attract government and foundation grants. Let me draw a more real and total picture and outline the subject so that it is somewhat more than a buzzword.

Ensembles' expenses are forever mounting and members of ensembles are always looking for ways to cover them and to continue to expand. Private funds will help until the concert fees begin to cover some of the costs, but you should realize that there's not a lot of "gold in them there chamber music hills." A large proportion of successful ensembles are organized as not-for-profit because this form of business allows for survival, credibility, and expanded activity. The bad news is that there are considerable legal and business responsibilities that go hand in hand with all the perks. Let's delve a bit deeper.

When a group decides to organize as a not-for-profit corporation, they are actually creating a separate legal entity apart from themselves. The advantage of this is that the members, directors, and officers are protected legally from personal liability for debts and obligations of the corporation. People will feel more comfortable about being involved with your organization if they know they can't be sued for its debts. Also, the fact that you went to the trouble to incorporate implies that you are permanent, serious, and stable. You thus have more credibility in the business world and greater chances of attracting funding.

Most ensembles who incorporate fall into the Type B category of corporations which are organized for charitable, educational, religious, scientific, literary, or cultural purposes, or for the prevention of cruelty to animals. You must, however, satisfy two requirements.

1. Your primary purpose must be not-for-profit. Any surplus of income over expenses can be used only for the not-for-profit purposes for which the organization was formed.

2. No members, directors, or officers may receive any distribution of assets, income, or profits beyond salaries for services rendered.

In order to incorporate, you will need a lawyer. If your ensemble can't afford a lawyer's fees, contact Volunteer Lawyers for the Arts (see Appendices). If you qualify, VLA will refer you to a volunteer attorney who will help you organize as a not-for-profit corporation and then apply for tax-exempt status.

Once you incorporate as a Type B not-for-profit corporation, you have the option of applying to the Internal Revenue Service for exemption from federal taxes* on the income you receive and on contributions. The IRS exempts these organizations from the obligation of these taxes because the activities of the not-for-profit corporation are in the public interest. To achieve tax exemption, an application must be filed with the IRS and it will take several months to process. If you qualify, you will be given the code number 501 (C)3. The two major advantages to this code classification are that you don't pay federal income tax and all contributors may deduct their contributions on their federal tax returns. This is a nice motivation for them to give you financial support.

Now that you're more familiar with some of the advantages of becoming a not-for-profit tax-exempt corporation, let me mention a few of the attendant responsibilities:

- Articles of Organization must be written and filed at the appropriate state offices.

- Bylaws (corporate rules) must be drawn up before you can apply for tax-exempt status.

- A Board of Trustees must be assembled, meetings held, and corporate minutes taken.

- Explicit reports must be filed with the IRS and other agencies.

---

*You may also qualify for exemption from state and local taxes as well as sales, payroll, or real-estate taxes. Consult your lawyer.

- The group's activities must be conducted in accordance with IRS regulations.

- The organization's activities that contribute to the public benefit must be maintained.

New or small groups who choose not to go to the time, expense, and trouble of incorporating themselves have an option of linking up with an "umbrella" organization—a larger, tax-exempt institution that can help them receive monies and possibly handle some of the accounting. Again, Volunteer Lawyers for the Arts can help you locate such a sponsoring organization in your area.

I have merely skimmed the surface of the not-for-profit, tax-exempt corporation. There are other options of organization that you should explore also to acquaint yourself with their pluses and minuses. I highly recommend the following books to get you started:

To Be or Not to Be: An Artist's Guide to Not-for-Profit Incorporation, published by Volunteer Lawyers for the Arts, 1560 Broadway, Suite 711, New York NY 10036.

Organizational Manual for Chamber Music Ensembles, by Lillian Helmen, published by Chamber Music America, 215 Park Ave., New York NY 10003.

GETTING STARTED WITH GRANTS

Grantsmanship takes know-how, talent, and a tremendous amount of work and research. If you or your arts project qualify for government or foundation support, you should, by all means, give it a good and thorough try. Let me help you get started by recommending a few books and programs, and by passing along the address and telephone numbers of the National Endowment for the Arts and the Foundation Center Collection nearest you.

To Read:

Des Marais, Philip. *How to Get Government Grants.* 2nd. Ed. New York: Public Service Materials Center, 1980.

Hillman, Howard. *The Art of Winning Goverment Grants.* New York: The Vanguard Press, Inc. 1979.

Hillman, Howard, and Abravanel, Karen. *The Art of Winning Foundation Grants.* New York: The Vanguard Press, Inc. 1975.

Kritz, Norton. *Program and Proposal Writing.* The Grantsmanship Center (see below).

Kurzig, Carol. *Foundation Fundamentals.* New York: The Foundation Center, 1980.

Also check your library for a reference copy of the *Catalogue of Federal Domestic Assistance.* This is an official U.S. government publication that describes all federal programs which offer funds.

To Investigate:
The Grantmanship Center offers three-to-five-day workshops in cities throughout the United States covering such topics as Grant Proposal Writing, Foundation and Corporate Funding, Grantsmanship Training and Business Ventures for Nonprofits. Each year over 300 workshops are conducted in more than 70 cities. To check the schedule for the workshop nearest you, call their toll-free number 800-421-9512. The Center also publishes a magazine (six times a year) called *The Grantsmanship Center News.* Important reprints from past issues are available, so call and request a catalogue from: The Grantsmanship Center, 1031 South Grand Avenue, Los Angeles CA 90015. (213)749-4721.

To Know About:
"The National Endowment for the Arts, an independent agency of the federal government, was created in 1965 to encourage and support American arts and artists. It fulfills its mission by awarding grants and through its leadership and advocacy activities."

This excerpt is from a publication called *Guide to the National Endowment for the Arts.* It will inform you about the agency and the programs of assistance and it's available from the Office of Public Affairs, The National Endowment for the Arts, 1100 Pennsylvania Ave., N.W., Washington DC 20506, (202)682-5400.

If you are an artist or organization eligible and planning to apply, guidelines to the different programs are available upon request. Write to the Music or Opera-Musical Theater Programs at the above addres. The phone number for the Music Program is (202)682-5445; the number for the Opera-Musical Theater Program is (202)682-5447.

Note: There are fellowships available for solo recitalists.

THE FOUNDATION CENTER

There are approximately twenty-six thousand foundations in this country which offer various kinds of support to individuals and groups. The Foundation Center collects and distributes information about them all via a nationwide network of library reference collections and publications. It is a service organization supported primarily by foundations.

Individual musicians would be particularly interested in the publication, *Foundation Grants to Individuals*. Nonprofit organizations should take a look at *The Foundation Directory*. So if you decide you need to attract funding from a private foundation, check the following pages for a library near you.

Local affiliate collections (*) provide a core collection of Center publications for free public use.

Some reference collections (●) are operated by foundations or area associations of foundations. They are often able to offer special materials or provide extra services, such as seminars or orientations for users, because of their close relationship to the local philanthropic community. All other collections are operated by cooperating libraries or other nonprofit agencies. Many are located within public institutions and all are open to the public during a regular schedule of hours.

You can telephone individual libraries for more information about their holdings or hours. To check on new locations call toll-free 800-424-9836 for current information. Here are some places to write or visit for information on foundation funding.

REFERENCE COLLECTIONS OPERATED BY THE FOUNDATION CENTER

The Foundation Center
888 Seventh Ave.
New York NY 10106
212-975-1120

The Foundation Center
1001 Connecticut Ave.
NW
Washington DC 20036
202-331-1400

The Foundation Center
Kent H. Smith Library
739 National City Bank Bldg.
619 Euclid
Cleveland OH 44114
216-861-1933

The Foundation Center
312 Sutter St.
San Francisco CA 94108
415-397-0902

COOPERATING COLLECTIONS

ALABAMA
Birmingham Public Library
2020 Park Pl.
Birmingham AL 35203
205-254-2541

Auburn University at Montgomery
Library
Montgomery AL 36193
205-279-9110

ALASKA
University of Alaska, Anchorage
Library
3211 Providence Dr.
Anchorage AK 99504
907-263-1848

ARIZONA
Phoenix Public Library
Social Sciences Subject Dept.
12 East McDowell Rd.
Phoenix AZ 85004
602-262-4782

Tucson Public Library
Main Library
200 South Sixth Ave.
Tucson AZ 85701
602-791-4393

ARKANSAS
Westark Community College Library
Grand Ave. at Waldron Rd.
Fort Smith AR 72913
501-785-4241

Little Rock Public Library
Reference Department
700 Louisiana St.
Little Rock AR 72201
501-370-5950

CALIFORNIA
● California Community Foundation
Funding Information Center
1151 West Sixth St.
Los Angeles CA 90017
213-413-4719

★Riverside Public Library
3581 7th St.
Riverside CA 92501
714-787-7201

★California State Library
Reference Services, Rm. 309
914 Capitol Mall
Sacramento CA 95814
916-322-0369

San Diego Public Library
820 E. St.
San Diego CA 92101
714-236-5816

Foundation Center
San Francisco Field Office
see address above

★Orange County
Community Development Council
1440 E. First St. 4th Floor
Santa Ana CA 92701
714-547-6801

Santa Barbara Public Library
Reference Section
40 East Anapamu
Box 1019
Santa Barbara CA 93102
805-962-7653

★Central Sierra Arts Council
19411 Village Dr.
Sonora CA 95370
209-532-2787

★North Coast Opportunities, Inc.
101 West Church St.
Ukiah CA 95482
707-462-1954

COLORADO
★Pikes Peak Library District
20 North Cascasde Ave.
Colorado Springs CO 80901
303-473-2080

Denver Public Library
Sociology Division
1357 Broadway
Denver CO 80203
303-571-2190

CONNECTICUT
Hartford Public Library
Reference Department
500 Main St.
Hartford CN 06103
203-525-9121

★D.A.T.A.
81 Saltonstall Ave.
New Haven CN 06513
203-776-0797

DELAWARE
Hugh Morris Library
University of Delaware
Newark NJ 19711
302-738-2965

FLORIDA
Jacksonville Public Library
Business, Science, and Industry
Department
122 North Ocean St.
Jacksonville FL 32202
904-633-3926

Miami-Dade Public Library
Florida Collection
One Biscayne Blvd.
Miami FL 33132
305-579-5001

★Leon County Public Library
Community Funding Resources
Center
1940 North Monroe St.
Tallahassee FL 32303
904-487-2665

★Orlando Public Library
10 North Rosalind
Orlando FL 32801
305-425-4694

GEORGIA
Atlanta Public Library
1 Margaret Mitchell Square at For-
syth and Carnegie Way
Atlanta GA 30303
406-688-4636

HAWAII
Thomas Hale Hamilton Library
General Reference
University of Hawaii
2550 The Mall
Honolulu HI 96822
808-948-7214

●★ Community Resource Center
The Hawaiian Foundation
Financial Plaza of the Pacific
111 S. King St.
Honolulu HI 96813
808-525-8548

IDAHO
Caldwell Public Library
1010 Dearborn St.
Caldwell ID 83605
208-459-3242

ILLINOIS

★Belleville Public Library
121 E. Washington St.
Belleville IL 62220
618-234-0441

● Donors Forum of Chicago
208 South LaSalle St.
Chicago IL 60604
312-726-4882

Sangamon State University Library
Shepherd Rd.
Springdale IL 62708
217-786-6633

INDIANA

★Allen County Public Library
900 Webster St.
Fort Wayne IN 46802
219-424-7241

★Indiana University Northwest Library
3400 Broadway
Gary IN 46408
219-980-6580

Indianapolis-Marion County Public Library
40 East St. Clair St.
Indianapolis IN 46204
317-269-1733

IOWA

Public Library of Des Moines
100 Locust St.
Des Moines IA 50308
515-283-4259

KANSAS

Topeka Public Library
Adult Services Department
1515 West Tenth St.
Topeka KS 66604
913-233-2040

★Wichita Public Library
223 South Main
Wichita KS 67202
316-262-0611

KENTUCKY

●★ The Louisville Community Foundation, Inc.
623 West Main St.
Louisville KY 40202
502-585-4649

Louisville Free Public Library
Fourth and York Sts.
Louisville KY 40203
502-584-4154

LOUISIANA

East Baton Rouge Parish Library
Centroplex Library
120 St. Louis St.
Baton Rouge LA 70802
504-344-5291

New Orleans Public Library
Business and Science Division
219 Loyola Ave.
New Orleans LA 70140
504-524-7382 ext. 33

★Shreve Memorial Library
424 Texas St.
Shreveport LA 71101
318-226-5894

MAINE

University of Southern Maine
Center for Research and Advanced Study
246 Deering Ave.
Portland ME 04102
207-780-4411

MARYLAND
Enoch Pratt Free Library
Social Science and History Department
400 Cathedral St.
Baltimore MD 21201
301-396-5320

MASSACHUSETTS
• Associated Grant-
makers of Massachusetts
294 Washington St.
Suite 501
Boston MA 02108
617-426-2608

Boston Public Library
Copley Square
Boston MA 02117
617-536-5400

★Walpole Public Library
Walcott Ave.
at Union St.
East Walpole MA 02032
617-668-0232

★Western Massachusetts
Funding Resource Center
Campaign for
Human Development
Chancery Annex,
73 Chestnut St.
Springfield MA 01103
413-732-3175 ext. 67

★Grants Resource Center
Worcester Public Library
Salem Square
Worcester MA 01608
617-799-1655

MICHIGAN
Alpena County Library
211 North First Ave.
Alpena MI 49707
517-356-6188

Henry Ford
Centennial Library
16301 Michigan Ave.
Dearborn MI 48126
313-943-2337

Purdy Library
Wayne State University
Detroit MI 48202
313-577-4040

Michigan State
University Libraries
Reference Library
East Lansing MI 48824
517-353-8816

★Farmington Community
Library
32737 West 12 Mile Rd.
Farmington Hills MI 48018
313-553-0300

University of Michigan-
Flint Library
Reference Department
Flint MI 48503
313-762-3408

Grand Rapids
Public Library
Sociology and
Education Dept.
Library Plaza
Grand Rapids MI 49503
616-456-4411

Michigan Technological
University Library
Highway U.S. 41
Houghton MI 49931
906-487-2507

MINNESOTA
Minneapolis Public Library
Sociology Department
300 Nicollet Mall
Minneapolis MN 55401
612-372-6555

★Saint Paul Public Library
90 West Fourth St.
Saint Paul MN 55102
612-292-6311

MISSISSIPPI
Jackson Metropolitan Library
301 North State St.
Jackson MS 39201
601-944-1120

MISSOURI
● Clearinghouse for
Mid-continent Foundations
Univ. of Missouri, Kansas City
Law School, Suite 1-300
52nd St. and Oak
Kansas City MO 64113
816-276-1176

● Metropolitan Association
for Philanthropy, Inc.
5600 Oakland, G-324
St. Louis MO 63110
314-647-2290

Springfield-Greene
County Library
397 East Central St.
Springfield IL 65801
417-866-4636

MONTANA
Eastern Montana
College Library
Reference Department
Billings MT 59101
406-657-2262

★Montana State Library
Reference Department
930 East Lyndale Ave.
Helena MT 59601
406-449-3004

NEBRASKA
W. Dale Clark Library
Social Sciences Department
215 South 15th St.
Omaha NE 68102
402-444-4822

NEVADA
Clark County Library
1401 E. Flamingo Rd.
Las Vegas NV 89109
702-733-7810

Washoe County Library
301 South Center St.
Reno NV 89505
702-785-4190

NEW HAMPSHIRE
● The New Hampshire
Charitable Fund
One South St.
Box 1335
Concord NH 03301
603-225-6641

★Littleton Public Library
109 Main St.
Littleton NH 03561
603-444-5741

NEW JERSEY
★The Support Center
744 Broad St., Suite 1106
Newark NJ 07102
201-643-5774

New Jersey State Library
Governmental Reference
185 West State St.
Box 1898
Trenton NJ 08625
609-292-6220

NEW MEXICO
New Mexico State Library
325 Don Gaspai St.
Santa Fe NM 87503
505-827-2033

NEW YORK
New York State Library
Cultural Education Center
Humanities Section
Empire State Plaza
Albany NY 12230
518-474-7645

Buffalo and Erie County
Public Library
Lafayette Square
Buffalo NY 14203
716-856-7525

Levittown Public Library
Reference Department
One Bluegrass La.
Levittown NY 11756
516-731-5728

Plattsburgh Public Library
Reference Department
15 Oak St.
Plattsburgh NY 12901
518-563-0921

Rochester Public Library
Business and Social
Sciences Divison
115 South Ave.
Rochester NY 14604
716-428-7328

Onondaga County
Public Library
335 Montgomery St.
Syracuse NY 13202
315-473-4491

NORTH CAROLINA
North Carolina State Library
109 East Jones St.
Raleigh NC 27611
919-733-3270

● The Winston-Salem Foundation
229 First Union
National Bank Bldg.
Winston-Salem NC 27101
919-725-2382

NORTH DAKOTA
★Western Dakota Grants
Resource Center
Bismarck Junior College Library
Bismarck ND 58501
701-224-5450

The Library
North Dakota State University
Fargo ND 58105
701-237-8876

OHIO
Public Library of Cincinnati
and Hamilton County
Education Department
800 Vine St.
Cincinnati OH 45202
513-369-6940

Foundation Center
Cleveland Field Office
see address above

★Ohio Dept. of Economic
and Community Development
Office of Grants Assistance
30 E. Broad St., 24th Flr.
Columbus OH 43215
614-466-6652

Toledo-Lucas County
Public Library
Social Science Department
325 Michigan St.
Toledo OH 43624
419-255-7055 ext. 221

OKLAHOMA
Oklahoma City
University Library
NW 23rd at North Blackwelder
Oklahoma City OK 73106
405-521-5072

Tulsa City-County
Library System
400 Civic Center
Tulsa OK 74103
918-592-7944

OREGON
Library Association
of Portland
Education and Documents,
Rm. 801
S.W. Tenth Ave.
Portland OR 97205
503-223-7201

PENNSYLVANIA
★Northampton County Area
Community College
Learning Resources Center
3835 Green Pond Rd.
Bethlehem PA 18017
215-861-5358

★Erie County
Public Library
3 South Perry Square
Erie PA 16501
814-452-2333 ext. 54

★Lancaster Public Library
125 North Duke St.
Lancaster PA 17602
717-394-2651

The Free Library
of Philadelphia
Logan Square
Philadelphia PA 19103
215-686-5423

Hillman Library
University of Pittsburgh
Pittsburgh PA 15260
412-624-4528

RHODE ISLAND
Providence Public Library
Reference Department
150 Empire St.
Providence RI 02903
401-521-7722

SOUTH CAROLINA
★Charleston County
Public Library
404 King St.
Charleston SC 29401
803-723-1645

South Carolina State Library
Reader Services Department
1500 Senate St.
Columbia SC 29211
803-758-3181

SOUTH DAKOTA
South Dakota State Library
State Library Bldg.
322 South Fort St.
Pierre SD 57501
605-773-3131

TENNESSEE
Knoxville-Knox County
Public Library
500 West Church Ave.
Knoxville TN 37902
615-523-0781

Public Library of
Nashville and Davidson County
8th Ave. N., and Union St.
Nashville TN 37203
615-244-4700

TEXAS
● The Hogg Foundation
for Mental Health
The University of Texas
Austin TX 78712
512-471-5041

Corpus Christi State
University Library
6300 Ocean Dr.
Corpus Christi TX 78412
512-991-6810

Dallas Public Library
Grants Information Service
1515 Young St.
Dallas TX 75201
214-749-4100

● El Paso
Community Foundation
El Paso National Bank Bldg.
Suite 1616
El Paso TX 79901
915-533-4020

★Funding Information Center
Texas Christian
University Library
Ft. Worth TX 76129
817-921-7000 ext. 6130

Houston Public Library
Bibliographic &
Information Center
500 McKinney Ave.
Houston TX 77002
713-224-5441 ext 265

Funding Information Library
1120 Milam Bldg.
115 E. Travis St.
San Antonio TX 78205
512-227-4333

UTAH
Salt Lake City Public Library
Business and Science Dept.
209 East Fifth St.
Salt Lake City UT 84111
801-363-5733

VERMONT
State of Vermont
Department of Libraries
Reference Services Unit
111 State St.
Montpelier VT 05602
802-828-3261

VIRGINIA
Grants Resources Library
Ninth Floor
Hampton City Hall
Hampton VA 23669
804-272-6496

Richmond Public Library
Business, Science and
Technology Department
101 East Franklin St.
Richmond VA 23219
804-780-8223

WASHINGTON
Seattle Public Library
1000 Fourth Ave.
Seattle WA 98104
206-625-4881

Spokane Public Library
Funding Information Center
West 906 Main Ave.
Spokane WA 99201
509-838-3361

WEST VIRGINIA
Kanawha County
Public Library
123 Capitol St.
Charleston WV 25301
304-343-4646

WISCONSIN
Marquette University
Memorial Library
1415 West Wisconsin Ave.
Milwaukee WI 53233
414-224-1515

WYOMING
Laramie County
Community College Library
1400 East College Dr.
Cheyenne WY 82001
307-634-5853

CANADA
● Canadian Centre for
Philanthropy
185 Bay St., Suite 504
Toronto Ont. Canada M56 1K6
416-364-4875

MEXICO
Biblioteca
Benjamin Franklin
Londres 16
Mexico City 6, D.F. Mexico
525-591-0244

PUERTO RICO
Universidad del
Sagrado Corazon
M.M.T. Guevarra Library
Correo Calle Loiza
Santurce PR 00914
809-728-1515 ext. 343

VIRGIN ISLANDS
College of the
Virgin Islands Library
Saint Thomas VI 00801
809-774-1252

RESOURCE BIBLIOGRAPHY

Arnold, Edmund C. *Ink on Paper.* 2nd ed. New York: Harper and Row, Publishers, Inc. 1972.

Cohen, Robert. *Acting Professionally.* 3rd ed. New York: Barnes & Noble Books, 1981.

Des Marais, Philip. *How to Get Government Grants.* 2nd ed. New York: Public Service Materials Center, 1980.

Emmons, Shirlee, and Sonntag, Stanley. *The Art of the Song Recital.* New York: Schirmer Books, 1979.

Fiedorek, Mary B. and Jewell, Diana Lewis. *Executive Style.* Piscataway, New Jersey: New Century Publishers, Inc., 1983.

Gould, J. Sutherland. *How to Publicize Yourself, Your Family, and Your Organization.* Englewood Cliffs, New Jersey: Prentice-Hall, Inc., 1983.

Gross, Sallie. *For Immediate Release: A Public Relations Manual.* Philadelphia: Greater Philadelphia Cultural Alliance, 1982.

Helmen, Lillian. *Organizational Manual for Chamber Music Ensembles.* New York: Chamber Music America, 1981.

Hillman, Howard. *The Art of Winning Government Grants.* New York: The Vanguard Press, Inc., 1979.

Hillman, Howard, and Abravanel, Karen. *The Art of Winning Foundation Grants.* New York: The Vanguard Press, Inc., 1975.

Hunt, Gordon. *How to Audition.* New York: Harper & Row, Publishers, Inc., 1977.

International Paper Company. *Pocket Pal: A Graphic Arts Production Handbook.* 13th ed. New York: IPC, 1983.

Levine, Mindy N., and Frank, Susan. *Get Me to the Printer On Time, On or Under Budget, and Looking Good.* New York: Off Off Broadway Alliance, 1981.

Maas, Jane. *Better Brochures, Catalogs, and Mailing Pieces.* New York: St. Martin's Press, 1981.

MacIntyre, Kate. *Sold Out.* New York: Theatre Development Fund, 1980.

McArthur, Nancy. *How to do Theatre Publicity.* Berea, Ohio: Good Ideas Company, 1977.

O'Brien, Richard. *Publicity: How to Get It.* New York: Harper & Row, Publishers, Inc., 1977.

Volunteer Lawyers for the Arts. *Fear of Filing.* New York: VLA, 1982.

Volunteer Lawyers for the Arts. *To Be or Not to Be: An Artist's Guide to Not-for-Profit Incorporation.* New York: VLA, 1982.

Whittlesey, Marietta. *Freelance Forever.* New York: Avon Books, 1982.

Wolf, Thomas. *Presenting Performances.* 4th ed. New York: American Council for the Arts, 1981.

INDEX

Other Books Of Interest

The Complete Book of Scriptwriting, by J. Michael Straczynski—Complete information on writing scripts for TV, radio, film, and theater—the rewards and pitfalls, working relationships, mechanics, and marketing. 265 pages/$14.95

How to Write a Play, by Raymond Hull—Advice on writing a performable play and getting it produced by one of the thousands of theater groups looking for new material, with practice exercises, a summary of theater history, a glossary of technical terms, and listings of publications for playwrights. 240 pages/$13.95

International Writers' & Artists' Yearbook—An annual directory of where to sell your music in English-speaking countries world-wide, with publishers subdivided by country. These listings, updated each year, tell what type of material is wanted and where and how to submit it. 530 pages/$10.95, paper

Making Money Making Music (No Matter Where You Live), by James Dearing—How to build a successful music career in your own community by playing clubs in solo or group acts, performing radio and TV jingles, operating a recording studio, teaching, and selling lyrics through the mail. Includes tips on getting a record contract. 320 pages/$12.95, paper

Songwriter's Market—2,000 listings of record companies/producers, music publishers, advertising agencies, play producers/publishers, and audiovisual companies purchasing songs—with contact name/address, pay rates, submission requirements, types of songs wanted. Includes interviews, articles, and business tips. Updated annually. 432 pages/$14.95

The TV Scriptwriter's Handbook, by Alfred Brenner—Here's how to write for television: where to get ideas; whom to sell and how to sell your script; what the format looks like; the role of the producer, editor, network executive, agent; contracts, fee structures, and residuals. 322 pages/ $12.95

A complete catalog of Writer's Digest Books may be obtained by writing to the address below.

To order directly from the publisher, include $1.50 postage and handling for one book, 50¢ for each additional book. Ohio residents add sales tax.

Send your order to: Writer's Digest Books, Department B
9933 Alliance Road
Cincinnati, Ohio 45242

Prices subject to change without notice.